An Unlikely Family

Voices of Ethiopian and American youth who are turning tragedy into hope

by
Ben Beisswenger
Christopher Beisswenger
Margaret Eldred
Zoe Dmitrovsky
Meron Foster
Carolynne Krusi

photographs by
Getu Tadesse
Jody Horan
and authors

Anemone Publishing Co.
2008

ISBN 9780975926413

First published November 2008 by Anemone Publishing Company
in the United States of America

To "Mom"
Carol Foster

This book is lovingly dedicated to Carol Foster, who, along with her husband Mike, has been the inspiration and the guiding force behind Selamta. She is warmly referred to as "Mom" not only by her own children, but by all the children of Selamta as well.

Acknowledgments

Generous contributions from The Byrne Foundation, Bill and Ann Brine, the Hyatt Family, the Abbey Family, George and Barbara Krusi and Marie Elise Young have made this book possible.

We gratefully acknowledge the fellowships received from the Tucker Foundation at Dartmouth College.

Special thanks to Abel Solomon, our outstanding translator, who allowed us to reach into each other's hearts.

Bray Mitchell's enthusiasm and technical support, both in Ethiopia and in the US, have been invaluable.

Thanks to Annemarie Linnehan for being able to answer all questions, and to Heidi Eldred for clarification of ideas, proofreading and help with marketing.

The administrative support that Getachew Ashagre provides for Selamta is essential to the success of the program, and his logistical help with the book project kept everything going smoothly.

Thanks to the Sisters of Each Other for their good humor and support.

As always, Barbara Jones' technical help and artistic advice kept us all on track.

And last, but certainly not least, many thanks to Paul Beisswenger for his limitless kindness and help, and for taking care of the myriad of small but essential things that he thinks no one notices.

Introduction

"An Unlikely Family" is an apt description of those brought together through the Selamta Children's Project in Addis Ababa, Ethiopia. Selamta represents a new community model for creating life-long families in order to repair a social fabric that has been ripped apart by the AIDS pandemic, poverty and despair.

In Ethiopia alone, there are over five million children orphaned by HIV/AIDS and other devastating circumstances. The most fortunate of these children are cared for by remaining family members who are themselves stretched beyond their means. But the overwhelming majority are separated from their siblings, and abandoned to the streets or into orphanages where they routinely encounter violence, predation and abuse. They are joined in poverty by millions of similarly marginalized elders and women who have lost their means of sustenance as their adult children and husbands are lost to AIDS.

The family structure that teaches care, respect and responsibility, and forms the foundation of a strong, productive society, has come apart in regions devastated by AIDS. What becomes of a nation and its people, when an entire generation is left to orphanages and the street? No amount of charity can overcome this tragedy. All the food in the world will not nourish children who are left to raise themselves. Education alone will not over-come the loss they suffer, nor can it impart the values absorbed within a family that offers safety, care and love.

Orphanages are not the answer because institu-tionalized food and shelter are only the most basic of human needs.

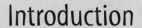

International adoption, though well intentioned, affects fewer than one percent of these children, and often leaves behind siblings and other family members, who deeply love them and grieve their loss. Adopted children also suffer from the loss of those left behind, and the sights, sounds and smells of their homeland.

If children are to become healthy, independent and productive adults, they need room to grow in a predictable home, supported by proper nutrition, health care, education and love. The Selamta Project is proving that these objectives are not beyond our reach. Over the past three years, we have learned the power of a simple formula:

* When a child arrives at the Selamta Center, they are welcomed into a large, warm family. Even among as many as fifty new brothers and sisters, they have their own clothes and possessions, the right to open the fridge and get a glass of milk, or grab a banana from the fruit bowl. These simple freedoms are powerful signals of inclusion and trust.

* Upon arrival, the Selamta staff immediately mobilizes to reunite the child with brothers and sisters, who may be scattered into different orphanages or living on the streets. We then try to locate extended family members, and bring them into the circle. Grandparents, aunts, uncles, cousins and family friends are all welcomed to the Center, and urged to become part of the children's lives again.

* For the first several months, our Selamta staff and US student "ambassadors" work to stabilize the child medically, nutritionally and emotionally. New children quickly realize that the environment is one of love and respect, and they learn to trust in the safety and joy of the Selamta family.

* As this healing takes place, we are welcoming new mothers into the Selamta Center, where they work with the children, and are educated thoroughly in parenting, health care and homemaking. These once-marginalized women will re-enter the community as new "moms" and "aunties" to a household of new brothers and sisters.

* Future families seem to gravitate into a shared orbit at Selamta Center. Soon, a mother and her group of eight to ten children emerge, and they are relocated as a new family into a clean, modern home nearby the Center. Selamta Families are not temporary or "foster" placements. They are brother and sister, son and daughter, nieces and nephews forever.

For the rest of the children's lives, there will always be someone to share joy and sorrow, turn to in times of need, and come home to visit for the holidays. And as they move through school and out into the world, the children will, in turn, do their best to provide support as their mom grows older. This is the traditional, sustainable circle of life, not only in Ethiopia, but in cultures across the world.

Selamta has proven the model. With minimal funding, and an entirely volunteer organization, Selamta is reuniting lost brothers and sisters, embracing disenfranchised women, creating vibrant, successful new families, and offering support that reaches deep into the surrounding community.

This book, "An Unlikely Family" is itself the result of these grassroots efforts. Authors Christopher, Margaret, Ben, Zoe and Meron represent dozens of young people who have now traveled to Ethiopia at their own expense, to experience the joy of working with Selamta's children. Each "ambassador" brings a project that will enrich the lives of our Selamta families or the broader community. Some have introduced arts and musical projects; others teach in the neighborhood schools, or develop the blueprints for sustainable businesses.

As you will see, these young authors have given voice to Ethiopian brothers, sisters, moms and aunties who join with American volunteers, to make up our "Unlikely Family." We are grateful for the love, laughter and fun they bring with them, and the remarkable contribution they share with our moms, aunties, staff, and the children of Selamta.

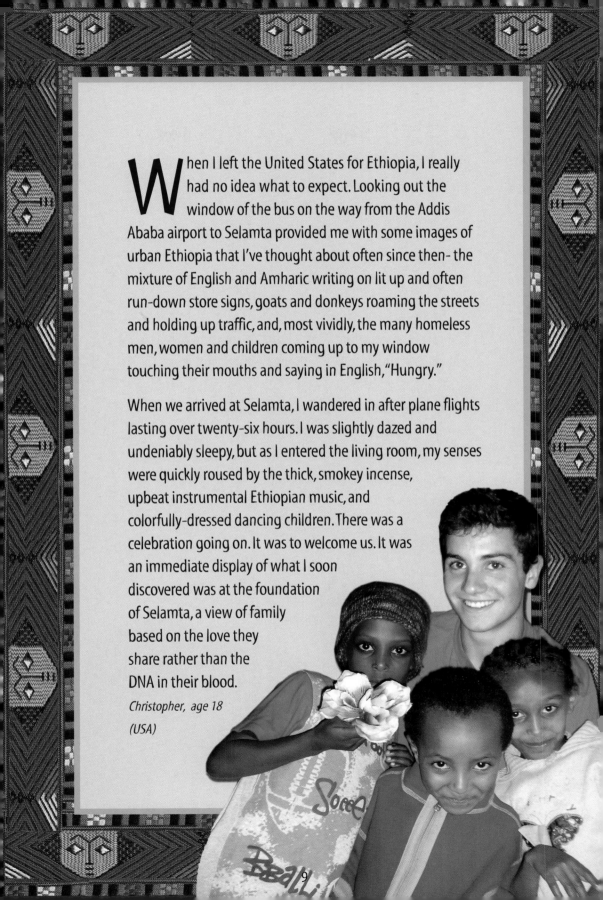

When I left the United States for Ethiopia, I really had no idea what to expect. Looking out the window of the bus on the way from the Addis Ababa airport to Selamta provided me with some images of urban Ethiopia that I've thought about often since then- the mixture of English and Amharic writing on lit up and often run-down store signs, goats and donkeys roaming the streets and holding up traffic, and, most vividly, the many homeless men, women and children coming up to my window touching their mouths and saying in English, "Hungry."

When we arrived at Selamta, I wandered in after plane flights lasting over twenty-six hours. I was slightly dazed and undeniably sleepy, but as I entered the living room, my senses were quickly roused by the thick, smokey incense, upbeat instrumental Ethiopian music, and colorfully-dressed dancing children. There was a celebration going on. It was to welcome us. It was an immediate display of what I soon discovered was at the foundation of Selamta, a view of family based on the love they share rather than the DNA in their blood.

Christopher, age 18

(USA)

9

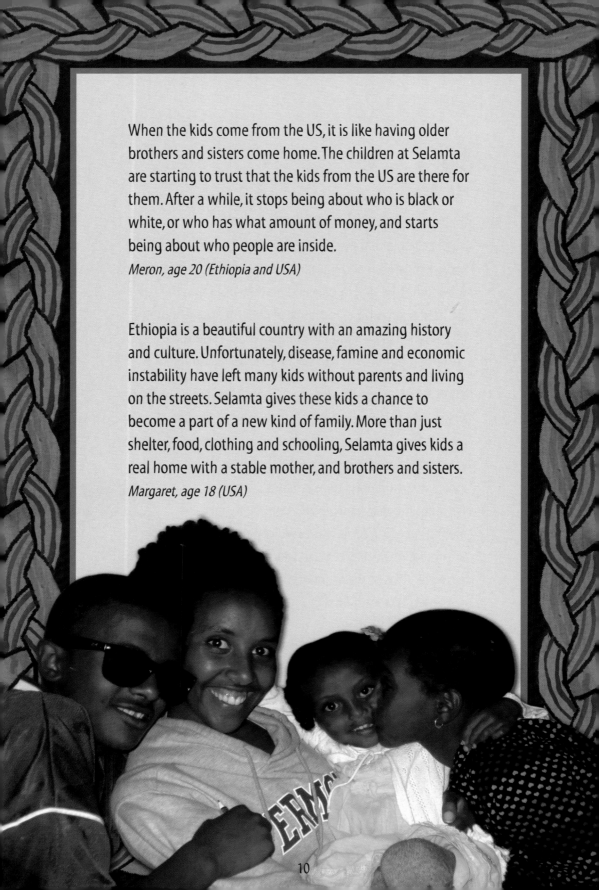

When the kids come from the US, it is like having older brothers and sisters come home. The children at Selamta are starting to trust that the kids from the US are there for them. After a while, it stops being about who is black or white, or who has what amount of money, and starts being about who people are inside.

Meron, age 20 (Ethiopia and USA)

Ethiopia is a beautiful country with an amazing history and culture. Unfortunately, disease, famine and economic instability have left many kids without parents and living on the streets. Selamta gives these kids a chance to become a part of a new kind of family. More than just shelter, food, clothing and schooling, Selamta gives kids a real home with a stable mother, and brothers and sisters.

Margaret, age 18 (USA)

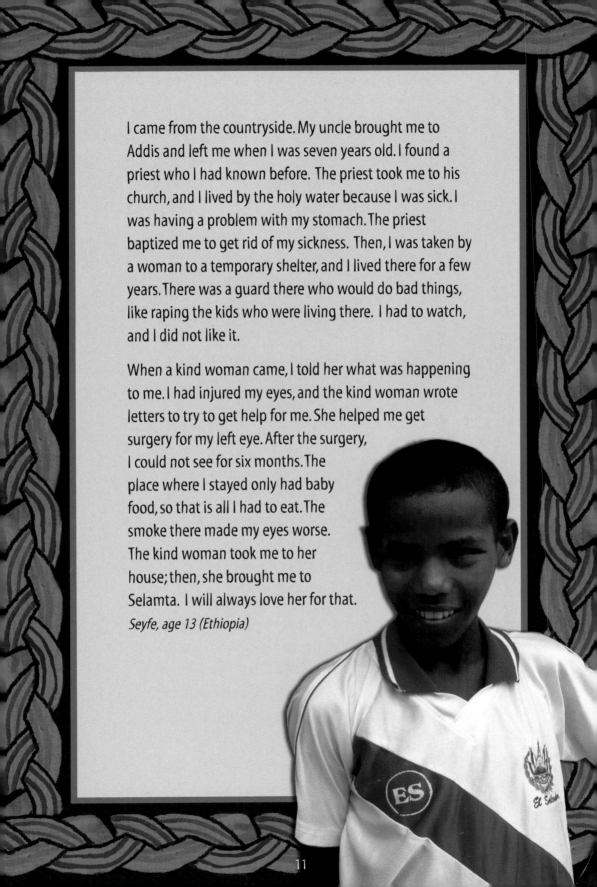

I came from the countryside. My uncle brought me to Addis and left me when I was seven years old. I found a priest who I had known before. The priest took me to his church, and I lived by the holy water because I was sick. I was having a problem with my stomach. The priest baptized me to get rid of my sickness. Then, I was taken by a woman to a temporary shelter, and I lived there for a few years. There was a guard there who would do bad things, like raping the kids who were living there. I had to watch, and I did not like it.

When a kind woman came, I told her what was happening to me. I had injured my eyes, and the kind woman wrote letters to try to get help for me. She helped me get surgery for my left eye. After the surgery, I could not see for six months. The place where I stayed only had baby food, so that is all I had to eat. The smoke there made my eyes worse. The kind woman took me to her house; then, she brought me to Selamta. I will always love her for that.

Seyfe, age 13 (Ethiopia)

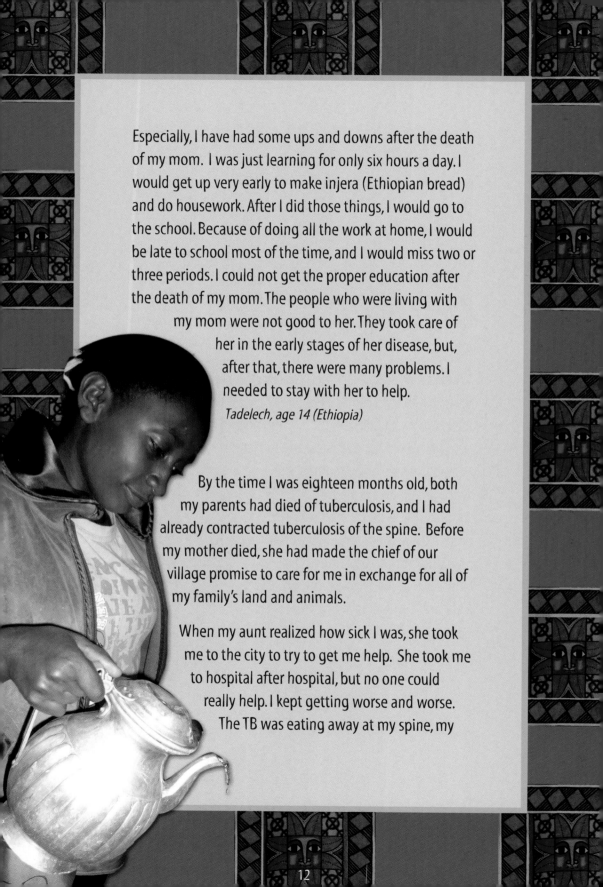

Especially, I have had some ups and downs after the death of my mom. I was just learning for only six hours a day. I would get up very early to make injera (Ethiopian bread) and do housework. After I did those things, I would go to the school. Because of doing all the work at home, I would be late to school most of the time, and I would miss two or three periods. I could not get the proper education after the death of my mom. The people who were living with my mom were not good to her. They took care of her in the early stages of her disease, but, after that, there were many problems. I needed to stay with her to help.

Tadelech, age 14 (Ethiopia)

By the time I was eighteen months old, both my parents had died of tuberculosis, and I had already contracted tuberculosis of the spine. Before my mother died, she had made the chief of our village promise to care for me in exchange for all of my family's land and animals.

When my aunt realized how sick I was, she took me to the city to try to get me help. She took me to hospital after hospital, but no one could really help. I kept getting worse and worse. The TB was eating away at my spine, my

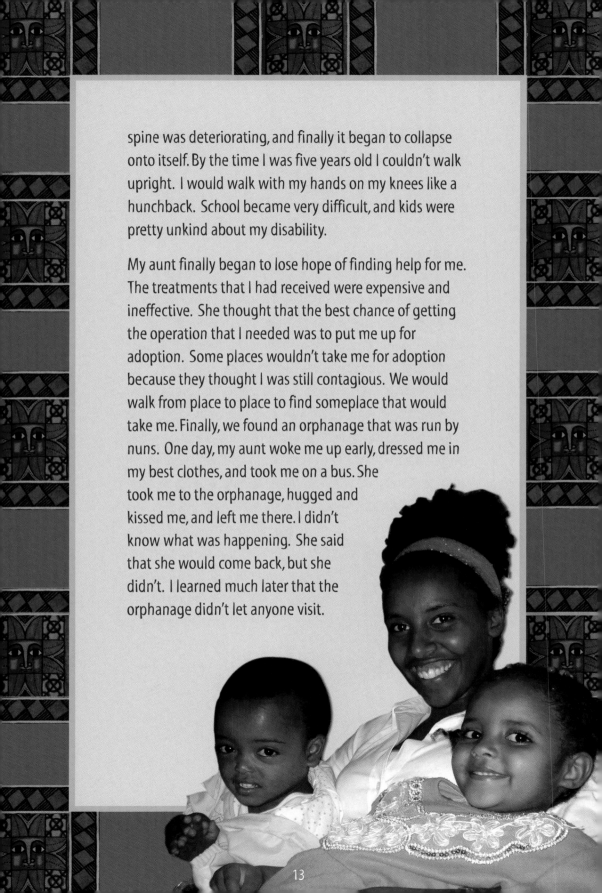

spine was deteriorating, and finally it began to collapse onto itself. By the time I was five years old I couldn't walk upright. I would walk with my hands on my knees like a hunchback. School became very difficult, and kids were pretty unkind about my disability.

My aunt finally began to lose hope of finding help for me. The treatments that I had received were expensive and ineffective. She thought that the best chance of getting the operation that I needed was to put me up for adoption. Some places wouldn't take me for adoption because they thought I was still contagious. We would walk from place to place to find someplace that would take me. Finally, we found an orphanage that was run by nuns. One day, my aunt woke me up early, dressed me in my best clothes, and took me on a bus. She took me to the orphanage, hugged and kissed me, and left me there. I didn't know what was happening. She said that she would come back, but she didn't. I learned much later that the orphanage didn't let anyone visit.

There was a lot of abuse, and no one would do anything about it. We were just the kids with no families. Kids got rabies because dogs would bite them. I had a dog bite that was left open for five days, and no one did anything. There was so much pain everywhere. It's pain that no one asked for. It's pain that kids can't handle.

A year later, I was moved to another orphanage. Everyone would try to look really cute so they would be chosen for adoption. I would try very hard to hide my disability. At that second orphanage, there was a lot of abuse. Kids were beaten, and girls were raped at night. The adults would leave the older boys in charge at night, and they would do terrible things to the other kids. If we told anyone, it would get much worse. I have always been outspoken. I told about everything I saw, and everyone who was hurt. The older boys would then torture me at night. They would pinch me, stick needles into me and crush my fingers. The problem with many orphanages is that they provide only food and shelter. What kids need is family. Selamta's mission is to create new families.

Meron, age 20 (Ethiopia and USA)

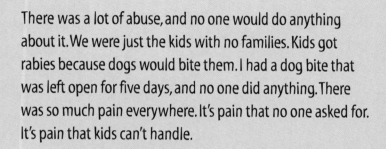

14

In Ethiopia, sometimes kids face situations that are not good for kids when they are growing up. When this happens, we need help. We need grown ups who can help us.   *Tigist, age 9 (Ethiopia)*

I remember when we went to pick up Dawit and Sentayehu. They were living in a cemetery, and there were people sleeping on the graves. They were wearing clothes that were much too small for them. They were really frightened when we came because they didn't know why we were there. There was an older woman who had been using the kids to beg for her, and it appeared to be her only source of money. There was lots of yelling when we tried to take the kids, which frightened the kids even more. I felt badly for the older woman, but the kids really needed to have a chance at a life of their own.

John, age 22 (USA)

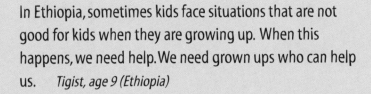

Dawit and Senayet as they
arrived at Selamta

When "Mom" came to pick up Sentayehu and me, we were
frightened. We didn't know where we were going. As we
were driving to Selamta, we saw a picture of Tsfanesh. We
knew her, and it made us feel better to know someone
where we were going. Senayet, my sister, didn't know
anything about what was happening because she was
living with an auntie. We told "Mom" about Senayet, and
they went to find her and bring her to be with us.
Dawit, age 8 (Ethiopia)

When "Mom" and the others came to take us to Selamta,
we had no idea what was happening to us. We were on our
way to the river to do our laundry, and someone was
calling us. I had saved 200 birr (about $20) to have my eye
fixed, and I was afraid that someone was going to take that
money away from me. When I found out that I could have
my eye fixed, and that I could save my 200 birr,
we decided to come to Selamta.
Sentayehu, age 13 (Ethiopia)

In the place we lived before Selamta, we
didn't get enough food, so we were
always hungry. We didn't have a chance to
go to school. Now we have plenty of food
and a chance to go to school. I will always
be happy about that.
Dawit, age 8 (Ethiopia)

I came from a place far away. When I lived there, the woman in charge ordered me to take care of all the other kids. "Mom" took me away from that, and brought me here so I could be a kid instead. I like to learn and I really appreciate the chance to do that.

Nardos, age 12 (Ethiopia)

When my mother and father died, there wasn't anyone to help me. There was conflict in my family. My relatives took my sisters because they were younger, but they wouldn't take me. I knew that I needed to find a way to be reunited with my sisters.

Fitsum, age 16 (Ethiopia)

Before I came to Selamta, I would wake up every morning and clean all the houses before I could go to school. When I came back from school, I cleaned more, or I worked in the place where they grind the teff. My sister, Fitsum, wasn't able to live with me, but when she got to Selamta, she came with Carol to pick me up so we could be together. I was surprised and very, very excited to see her.

Kidist, age 13 (Ethiopia)

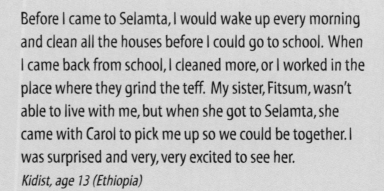

Early in my time in Ethiopia, I went to help pick up many of the kids who were coming to Selamta for their first time. I would go wherever the kids were living, be it on the streets in the city, a house that was owned by their recently deceased parents, or a relative's house. It was always tough to see where these kids came from because, while I was living at Selamta, I got used to seeing kids doing really well in a great environment. It was so easy for me to forget that all of our kids were once like the kids I was going to pick up.

It's a lot to wrap my mind around, for instance, that Nardos would be blind right now if she had not come to Selamta. I've seen pictures of her from before she came, and I barely recognize her. But still those were just pictures.

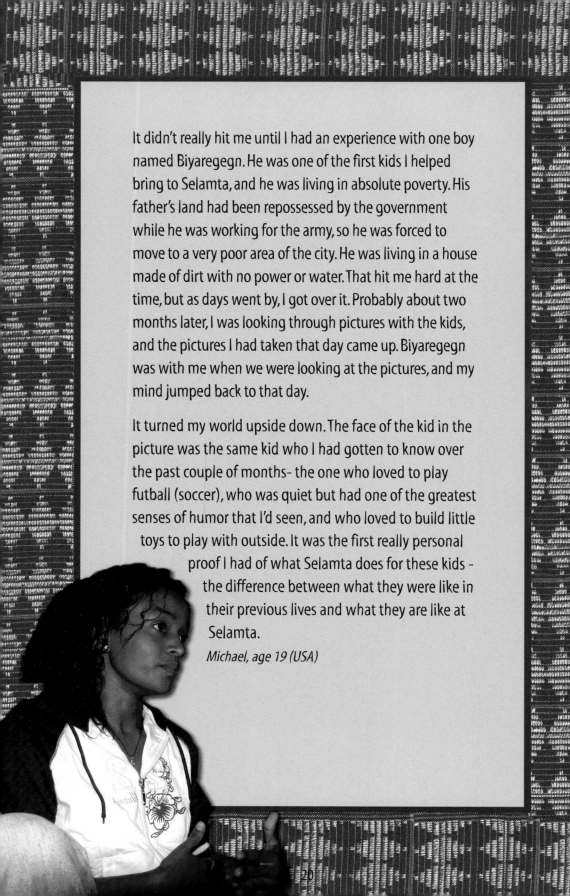

It didn't really hit me until I had an experience with one boy named Biyaregegn. He was one of the first kids I helped bring to Selamta, and he was living in absolute poverty. His father's land had been repossessed by the government while he was working for the army, so he was forced to move to a very poor area of the city. He was living in a house made of dirt with no power or water. That hit me hard at the time, but as days went by, I got over it. Probably about two months later, I was looking through pictures with the kids, and the pictures I had taken that day came up. Biyaregegn was with me when we were looking at the pictures, and my mind jumped back to that day.

It turned my world upside down. The face of the kid in the picture was the same kid who I had gotten to know over the past couple of months- the one who loved to play futball (soccer), who was quiet but had one of the greatest senses of humor that I'd seen, and who loved to build little toys to play with outside. It was the first really personal proof I had of what Selamta does for these kids - the difference between what they were like in their previous lives and what they are like at Selamta.

Michael, age 19 (USA)

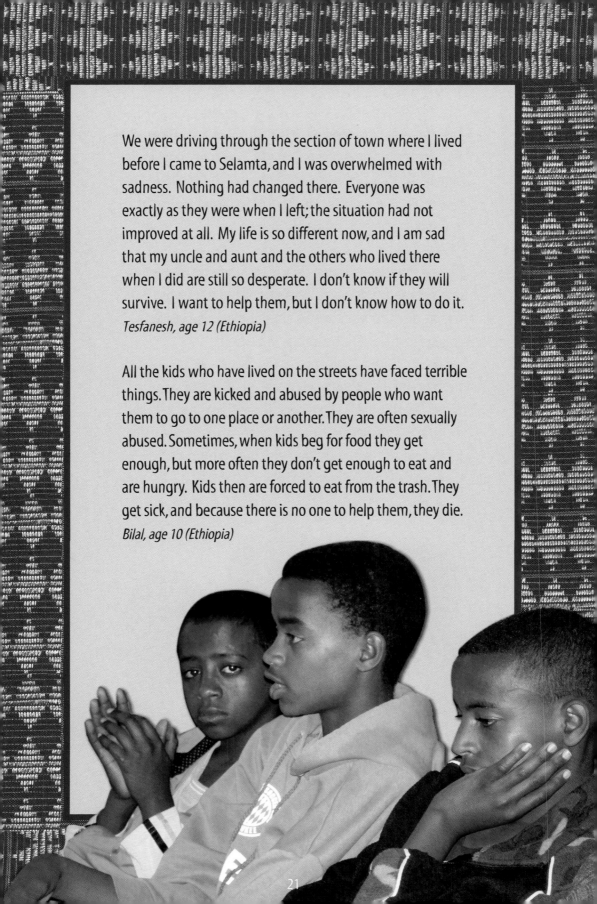

We were driving through the section of town where I lived before I came to Selamta, and I was overwhelmed with sadness. Nothing had changed there. Everyone was exactly as they were when I left; the situation had not improved at all. My life is so different now, and I am sad that my uncle and aunt and the others who lived there when I did are still so desperate. I don't know if they will survive. I want to help them, but I don't know how to do it.
Tesfanesh, age 12 (Ethiopia)

All the kids who have lived on the streets have faced terrible things. They are kicked and abused by people who want them to go to one place or another. They are often sexually abused. Sometimes, when kids beg for food they get enough, but more often they don't get enough to eat and are hungry. Kids then are forced to eat from the trash. They get sick, and because there is no one to help them, they die.
Bilal, age 10 (Ethiopia)

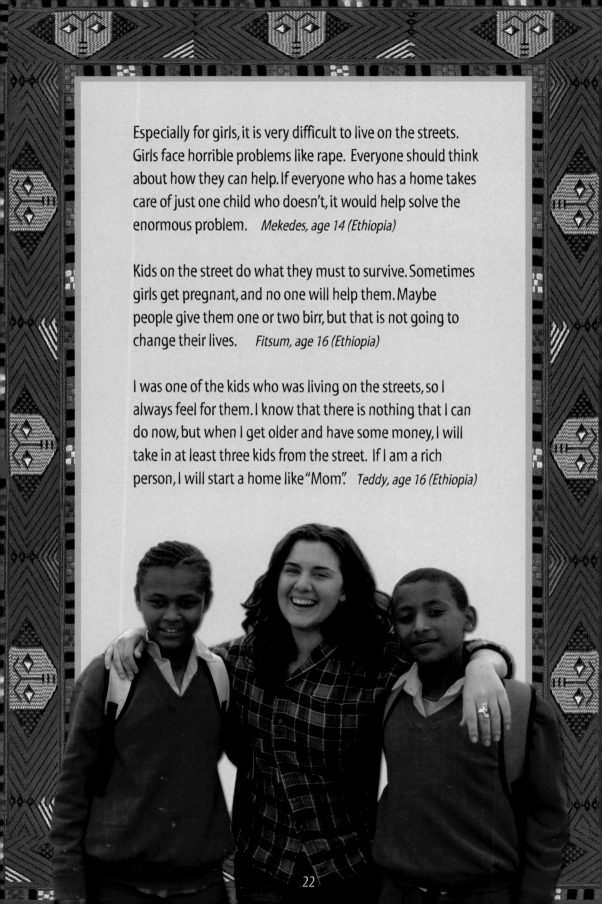

Especially for girls, it is very difficult to live on the streets. Girls face horrible problems like rape. Everyone should think about how they can help. If everyone who has a home takes care of just one child who doesn't, it would help solve the enormous problem. *Mekedes, age 14 (Ethiopia)*

Kids on the street do what they must to survive. Sometimes girls get pregnant, and no one will help them. Maybe people give them one or two birr, but that is not going to change their lives. *Fitsum, age 16 (Ethiopia)*

I was one of the kids who was living on the streets, so I always feel for them. I know that there is nothing that I can do now, but when I get older and have some money, I will take in at least three kids from the street. If I am a rich person, I will start a home like "Mom". *Teddy, age 16 (Ethiopia)*

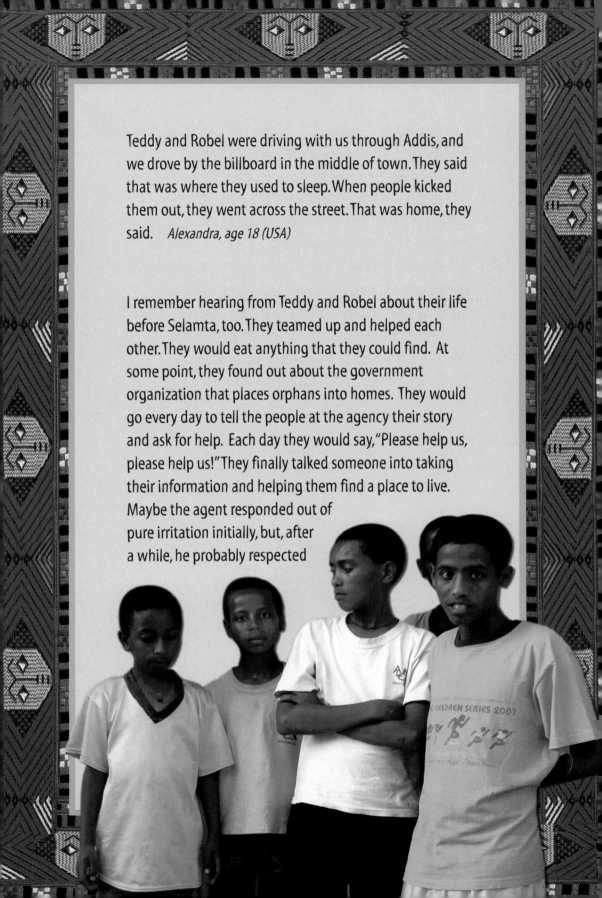

Teddy and Robel were driving with us through Addis, and we drove by the billboard in the middle of town. They said that was where they used to sleep. When people kicked them out, they went across the street. That was home, they said.   *Alexandra, age 18 (USA)*

I remember hearing from Teddy and Robel about their life before Selamta, too. They teamed up and helped each other. They would eat anything that they could find. At some point, they found out about the government organization that places orphans into homes. They would go every day to tell the people at the agency their story and ask for help. Each day they would say, "Please help us, please help us!" They finally talked someone into taking their information and helping them find a place to live. Maybe the agent responded out of pure irritation initially, but, after a while, he probably respected

them for trying to better their situation. All they needed was for the agency to help a little. That is how they found their way to Selamta.

While they lived on the streets, Teddy and Robel had to fend for themselves. Of all the kids at Selamta, they are the ones most conscious of how it is on the streets. When we are driving through town, their faces are glued to the window. They know every part of the city because they used to roam it on their own. They call each other brothers, and the way they care for each other is like brothers. *Meron, age 20 (Ethiopia and USA)*

The homeless kids need help from others to solve the problem. If people in other countries want to help, they should try to understand the kids. *Adisu, age 10 (Ethiopia)*

Children are at the world's mercy. These children were placed into a world where their only bed is the sidewalk. They have no choice. There are people who blame them for their situation. I don't understand that.

Alexandra, age 18 (USA)

One important way people could help the homeless kids living on the streets is to change their own attitudes. Many people blame the kids on the street for the circumstances that got them there. It was not their fault. People are afraid of those with HIV/AIDS and make negative judgments. That makes the situation worse for everyone. The first way for people to help is to change their attitudes about the people in need. After that, we need help creating places for kids to live, like Selamta. If they can't do it alone, they could work with others who want to help.   *Tizita, age 9 (Ethiopia)*

We are kids, and we cannot solve all these problems ourselves. We need help.   *Fitsum, age 16 (Ethiopia)*

When I see the kids on the streets, I feel so strongly for them. I know that they are the kids who I would be with if it had not been for Selamta. I know how important it is to help them. If they have the opportunity that I have had, they will survive.   *Belay, age 16 (Ethiopia)*

Kids on the street cannot survive without help from people like "Mom" and places like Selamta.
Adisu, age 10 (Ethiopia)

I think that people are afraid that kids who live on the streets might be HIV positive, so they don't want to accept them or help them.   *Tizita, age 9 (Ethiopia)*

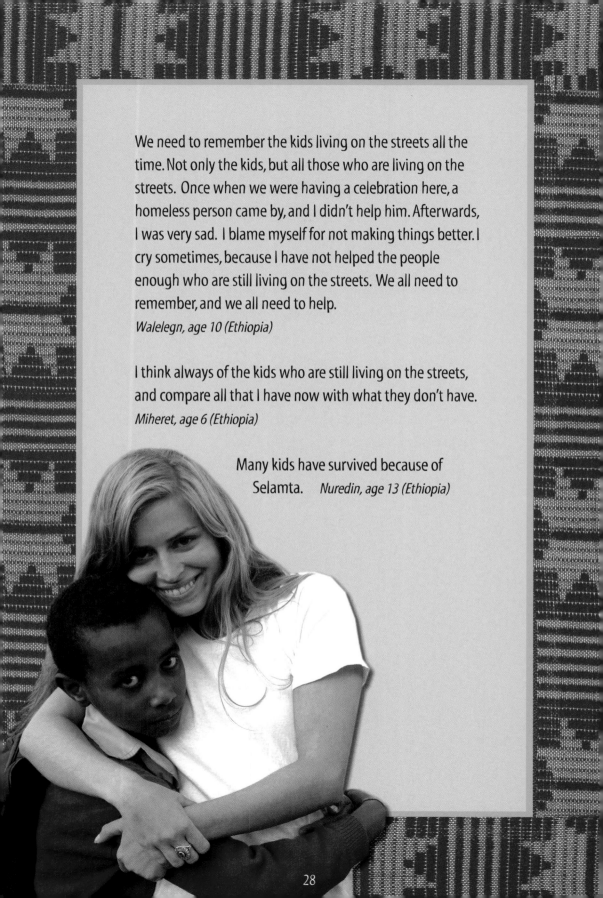

We need to remember the kids living on the streets all the
time. Not only the kids, but all those who are living on the
streets. Once when we were having a celebration here, a
homeless person came by, and I didn't help him. Afterwards,
I was very sad. I blame myself for not making things better. I
cry sometimes, because I have not helped the people
enough who are still living on the streets. We all need to
remember, and we all need to help.

Walelegn, age 10 (Ethiopia)

I think always of the kids who are still living on the streets,
and compare all that I have now with what they don't have.

Miheret, age 6 (Ethiopia)

Many kids have survived because of
Selamta.   *Nuredin, age 13 (Ethiopia)*

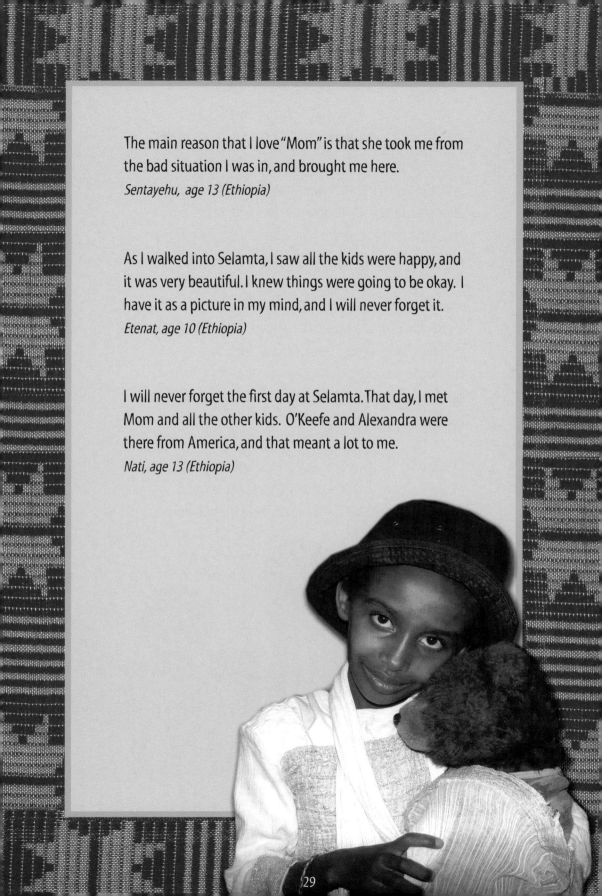

The main reason that I love "Mom" is that she took me from the bad situation I was in, and brought me here.

Sentayehu, age 13 (Ethiopia)

As I walked into Selamta, I saw all the kids were happy, and it was very beautiful. I knew things were going to be okay. I have it as a picture in my mind, and I will never forget it.

Etenat, age 10 (Ethiopia)

I will never forget the first day at Selamta. That day, I met Mom and all the other kids. O'Keefe and Alexandra were there from America, and that meant a lot to me.

Nati, age 13 (Ethiopia)

For some reason, I expected my travels in Ethiopia to be largely depressing. I knew that one out of six Ethiopians is infected with HIV/AIDS and that TB and other curable diseases are silent killers across the African continent. I expected these issues to play a prominent role in my daily experiences in Ethiopia. I anticipated these conflicts within the country to shape my reactions to my experience of living with the orphans. Selamta, however, is far from what I imagined an orphanage to be like, and I left Ethiopia feeling up-lifted. At Selamta, I saw firsthand the power of family to cultivate both love and happiness in a people who live simply and are aware of their country's political and social conflicts.   *Zoe, age 21 (USA)*

Living with their new families in the houses is a change for all the kids, but it seems to have made the biggest difference for the kids who have come from the most

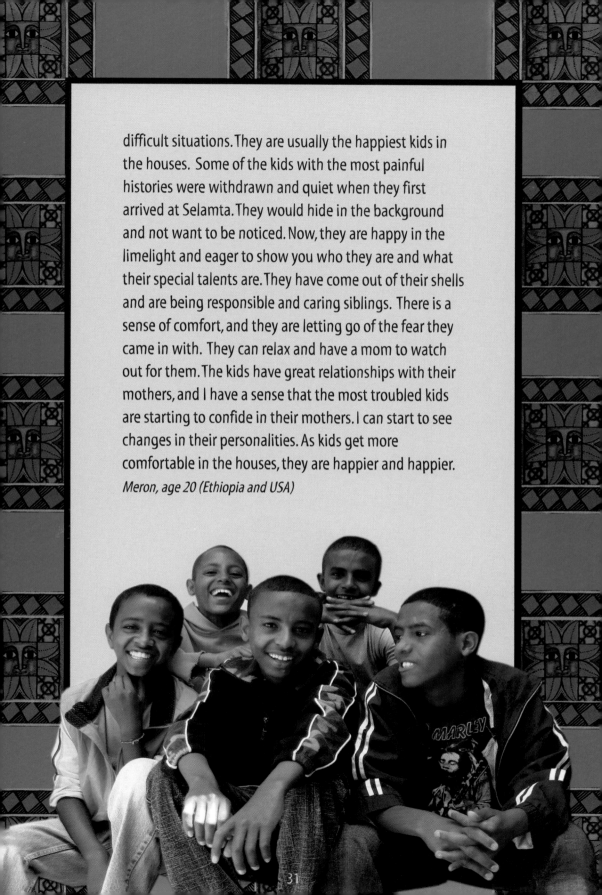

difficult situations. They are usually the happiest kids in the houses. Some of the kids with the most painful histories were withdrawn and quiet when they first arrived at Selamta. They would hide in the background and not want to be noticed. Now, they are happy in the limelight and eager to show you who they are and what their special talents are. They have come out of their shells and are being responsible and caring siblings. There is a sense of comfort, and they are letting go of the fear they came in with. They can relax and have a mom to watch out for them. The kids have great relationships with their mothers, and I have a sense that the most troubled kids are starting to confide in their mothers. I can start to see changes in their personalities. As kids get more comfortable in the houses, they are happier and happier.

Meron, age 20 (Ethiopia and USA)

It is amazing to watch how the mothers in each house devote themselves to their families at Selamta. They have a warmth about them, making everyone who enters their homes feel immediately like part of the family.
Ben, age 21 (USA)

Someone who truly cares about me is there when I am in trouble and when things are going well. On the good days and the bad days, I have someone to share my life with me. I can see that someone cares about me when they share everything with me. *Bilal, age 10 (Ethiopia)*

When someone shares his ideas with me, and not only talks with me, but also really listens to me, I feel loved. Love cannot be expressed by giving things. Just because someone gives me something, I cannot say that he loves me. But if he loves me, he will share with me from his heart. *Adisu, age 10 (Ethiopia)*

I can tell that someone really cares about me when they give me good advice. They take the time to help me.
Tigist, age 13 (Ethiopia)

I love Selamta because the ambassadors come to be with us.
Yohanes, age 11 (Ethiopia)

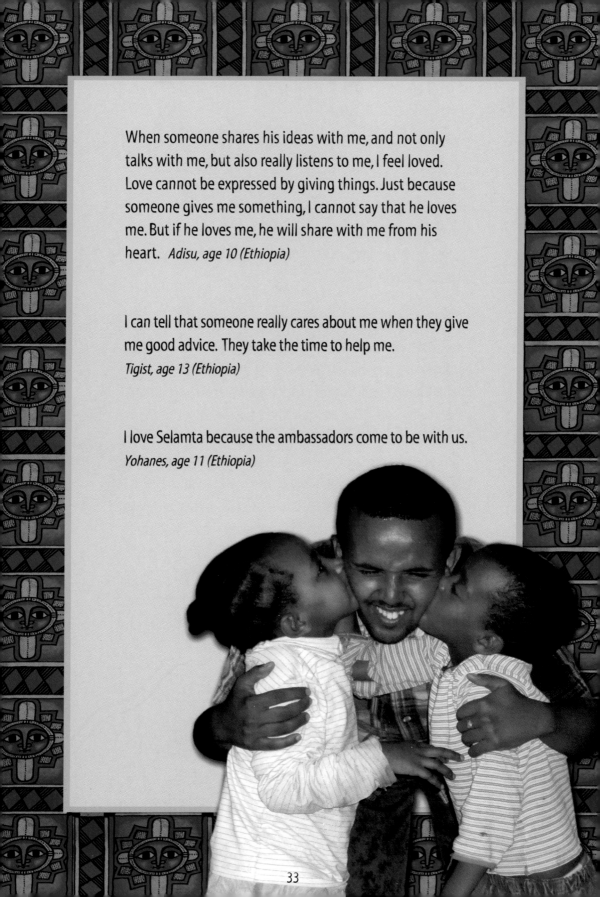

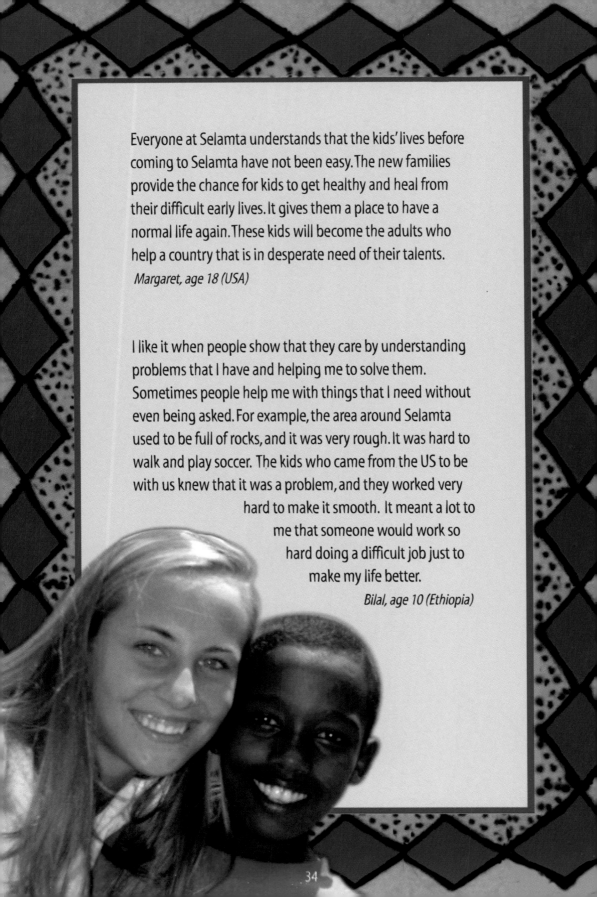

Everyone at Selamta understands that the kids' lives before coming to Selamta have not been easy. The new families provide the chance for kids to get healthy and heal from their difficult early lives. It gives them a place to have a normal life again. These kids will become the adults who help a country that is in desperate need of their talents.

Margaret, age 18 (USA)

I like it when people show that they care by understanding problems that I have and helping me to solve them. Sometimes people help me with things that I need without even being asked. For example, the area around Selamta used to be full of rocks, and it was very rough. It was hard to walk and play soccer. The kids who came from the US to be with us knew that it was a problem, and they worked very hard to make it smooth. It meant a lot to me that someone would work so hard doing a difficult job just to make my life better.

Bilal, age 10 (Ethiopia)

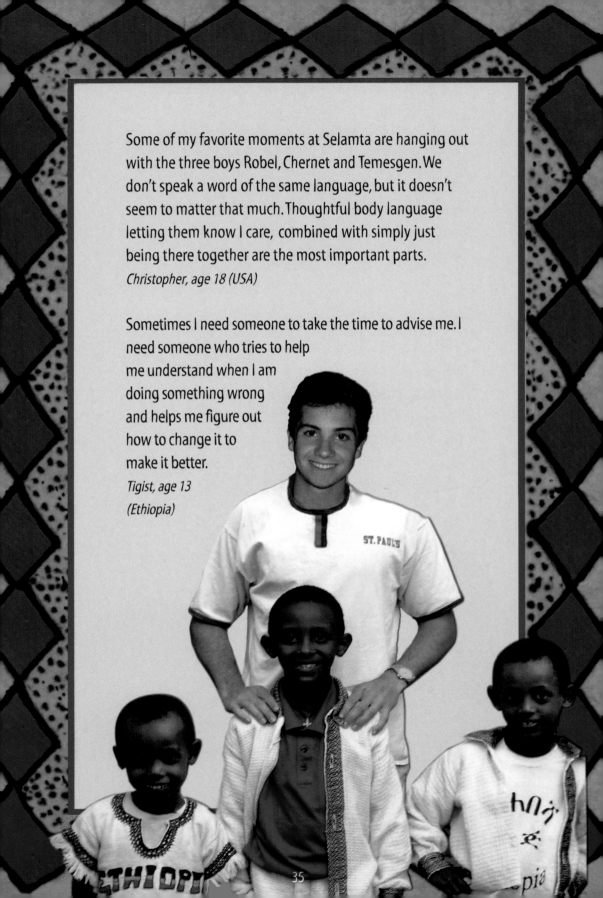

Some of my favorite moments at Selamta are hanging out with the three boys Robel, Chernet and Temesgen. We don't speak a word of the same language, but it doesn't seem to matter that much. Thoughtful body language letting them know I care, combined with simply just being there together are the most important parts.
Christopher, age 18 (USA)

Sometimes I need someone to take the time to advise me. I need someone who tries to help me understand when I am doing something wrong and helps me figure out how to change it to make it better.
Tigist, age 13 (Ethiopia)

When one of the kids is upset or worried about something, it doesn't go unnoticed. The well being of each person really matters at Selamta, so people pay attention not only the overt signs, but to the more subtle ones as well. People care, and they make a special effort to talk with the kids who are having a tough time.   *Julie, age 18 (USA)*

The kids from the US came here from a long way away to help us with everything that they can. And also, they learn about us and know us before they come here. By knowing us and by loving us, they give us all they can, so we consider them members of our family.

Getu, age 15 (Ethiopia)

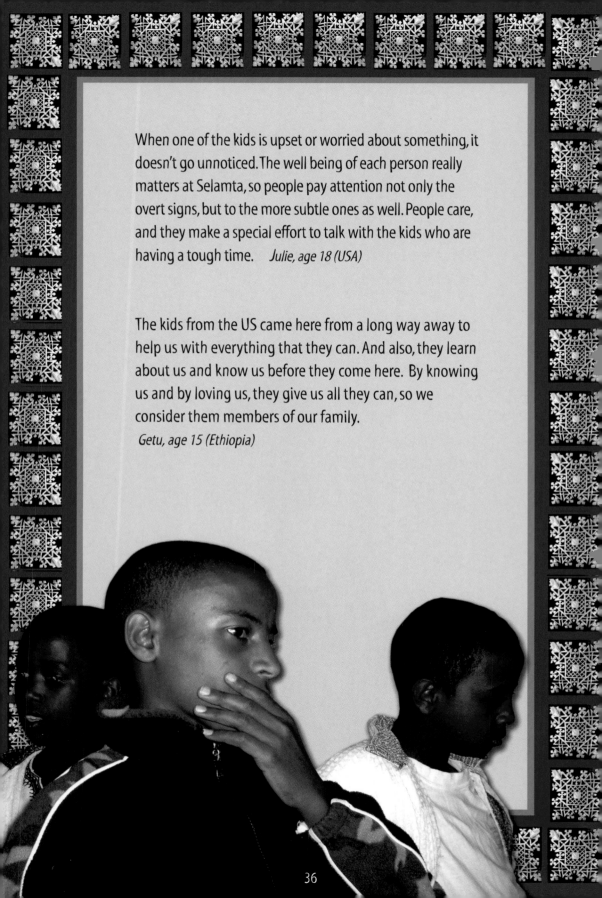

The American kids bring to Selamta the reminder that there are people out there who care and are willing to help. *Johnny, age 19 (USA)*

When people live and sleep and eat together, they form a family. *Hailu, age 7 (Ethiopia)*

I agree. Living and playing together, and loving each other makes a family. *Beemnet, age 9 (Ethiopia)*

Also, there needs to be respect between the people who are living together to make a family. And if I have something more than others in my family, I should share with them. *Walelegn, age 10 (Ethiopia)*

Whether or not we are related by blood,
if we are living under the same roof,
and we love and respect each other,
we are a family. *Robel, age 15 (Ethiopia)*

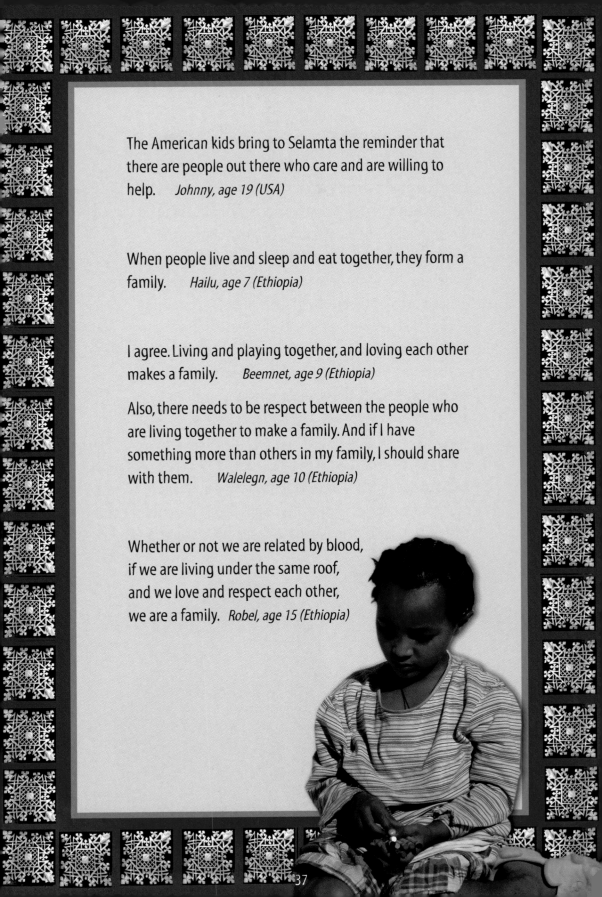

When kids come off the streets, they have often learned a
lot of behaviors that are not good for living in a group, but
they need them to survive on the streets. Sometimes kids
have to beg and steal to eat. Sometimes they have to do
worse things. For a lot of kids, it is hard to change the
behavior when they no longer need it. For Teddy and
Robel, the move into Selamta seemed effortless. No one
needed to teach them how to share or how to listen. The
younger kids look up to them. They have a special role at
Selamta, and they show the little kids how to share. They
are the older siblings; they play with the younger kids and
are silly with them. The younger kids light up when they
see them.   *Meron, age 20 (Ethiopia and USA)*

Being at Selamta and recognizing what the Ethiopian
orphans face makes most of the things that kids consider a
crisis in the US seem miniscule. Kids in the US think that if

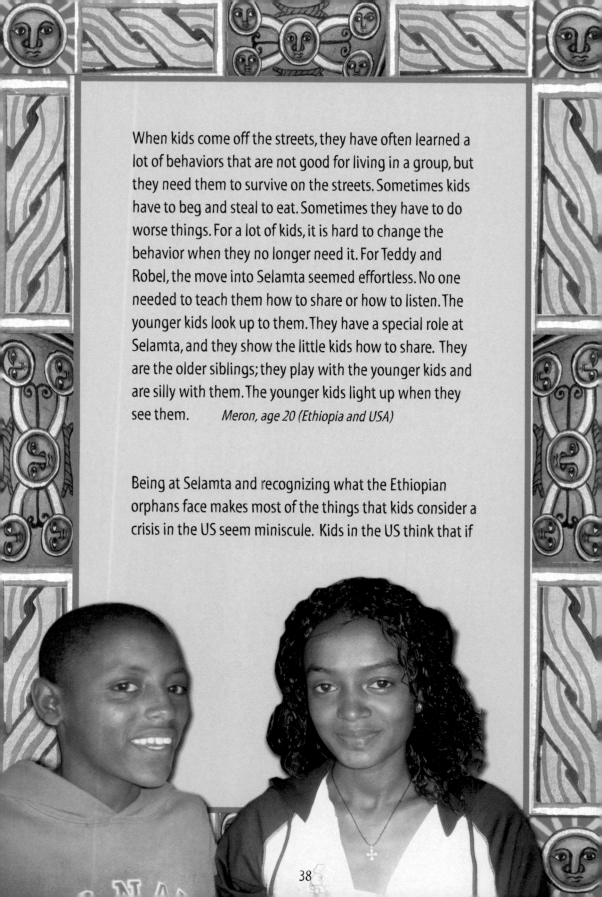

they aren't allowed to go out with their friends on a given night, it is a big deal. When you have seen the things that kids have to deal with in Ethiopia, it is hard to take that kind of thing seriously. *Johnny, 19 (USA)*

When I think of my mom and dad and that they are not with me now, it makes me hurt inside. My father died when I was four, and my mother died when I was in 5th grade. I think of them always. *Mekedes, age 14 (Ethiopia)*

Mekedes was very sad one day and having a hard time. She asked me just to sit by her and be with her. We just sat together, and I held her all day. Sometimes you don't need words. Just being there is important.
Alexandra, age 18 (USA)

I never had a chance to say good-bye to aunt and uncle. My brother and sister cannot be with me, and I was afraid I wouldn't see them again. I didn't talk for several days, and I couldn't tell people how sad I was.
Mulu, age 10 (Ethiopia)

My greatest sadness was when my family died, especially my father. *Meskerem, age 13 (Ethiopia)*

I was sad when my mom and my uncle were both sick together. I felt alone. *Miheret, age 8 (Ethiopia)*

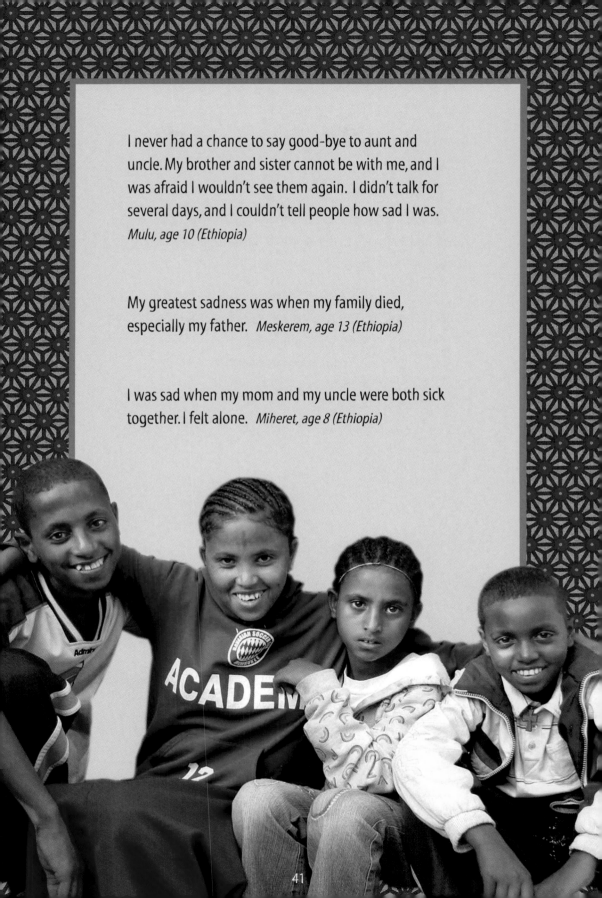

It was really hard for me when my mom was sick, too.
Tizita, age 9 (Ethiopia)

I am always sad that I was never able to see my mom. I never had a chance to get to know her since I was born.
Etenat, age 10 (Ethiopia)

I only saw my father once. I will always wish that I could have seen him again.
Tizita, age 9 (Ethiopia)

Nothing can replace a child's birth family and parents. When AIDS or other diseases take the lives of parents, kids are often forced to become adults before they are ready.
Margaret, age 18 (USA)

My greatest sadness is that my parents died before they had a chance to see what I would become. They will never know who I am now. *Nati, age 13 (Ethiopia)*

I feel the same way. I was sad when my mother died. I miss my mother so much. I lived with my aunt, but I always missed my mom. *Endriyas, 13 (Ethiopia)*

I am always unhappy when there is fighting in a family. I don't like it when people make arguments.
Eyob, age 11 (Ethiopia)

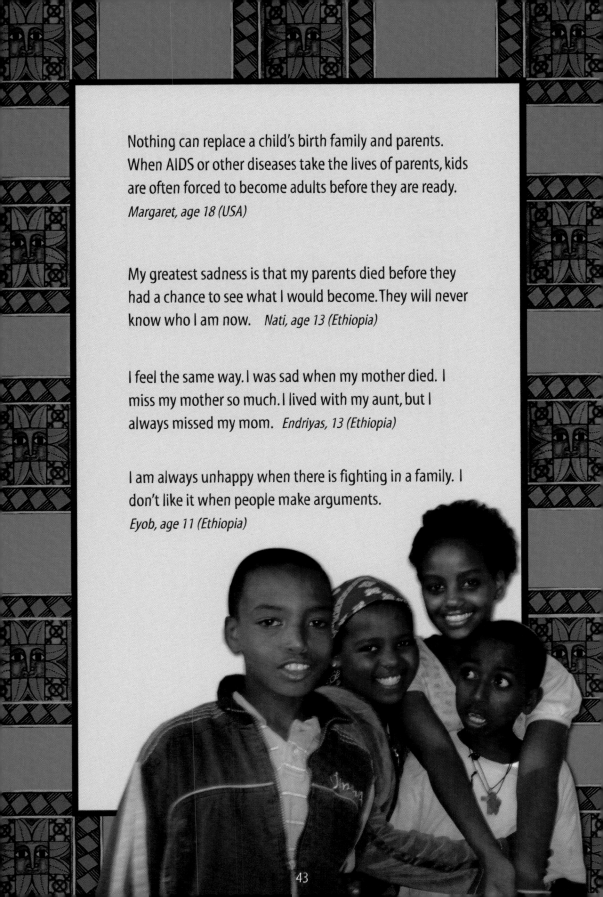

I have a hurt that always stays with me. I cannot live with my brothers and sister. I would do anything to be able to live with them. They are living in an SOS home, but I am too old, so they would not take me there. I miss them every day.

Adisu, age 10 (Ethiopia

Before I came to Selamta, I was living with an Auntie. I was afraid to leave her, so I refused to go. Then, someone told me I would have many brothers and sisters here. Now I am very glad that I came to Selamta.

Bethlehem, age 13 (Ethiopia and USA)

My father's death is always a source of sadness to me.

Nuredin, age 13 (Ethiopia)

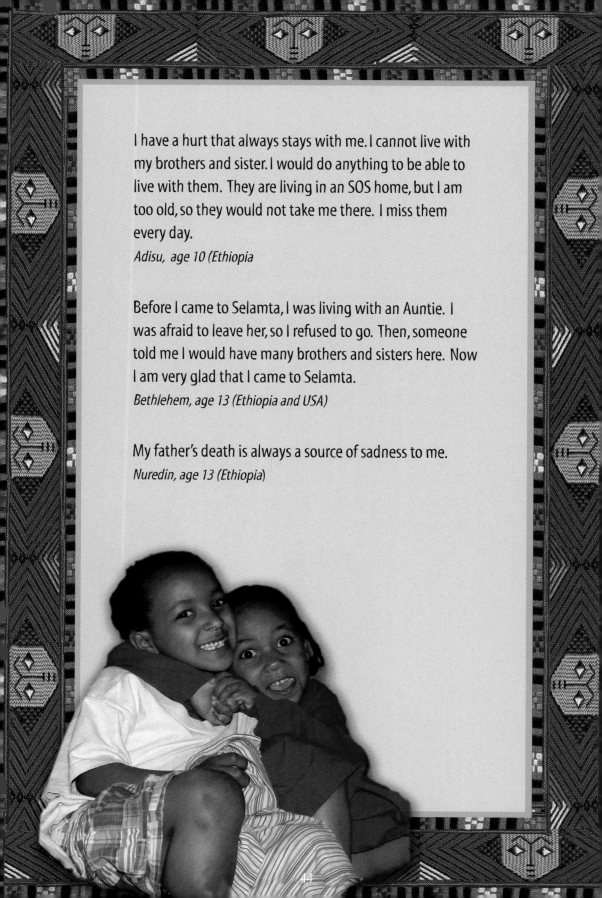

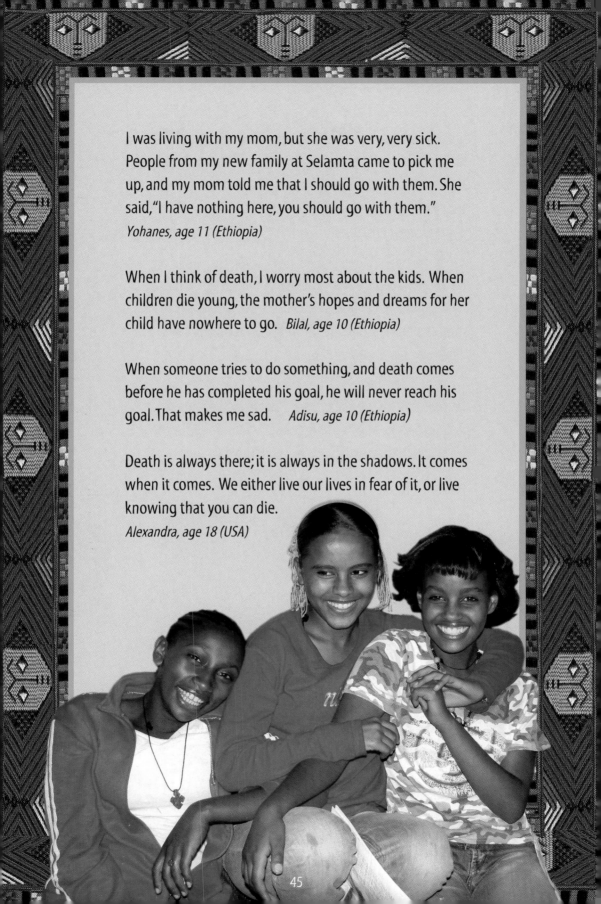

I was living with my mom, but she was very, very sick. People from my new family at Selamta came to pick me up, and my mom told me that I should go with them. She said, "I have nothing here, you should go with them."
Yohanes, age 11 (Ethiopia)

When I think of death, I worry most about the kids. When children die young, the mother's hopes and dreams for her child have nowhere to go. *Bilal, age 10 (Ethiopia)*

When someone tries to do something, and death comes before he has completed his goal, he will never reach his goal. That makes me sad. *Adisu, age 10 (Ethiopia)*

Death is always there; it is always in the shadows. It comes when it comes. We either live our lives in fear of it, or live knowing that you can die.
Alexandra, age 18 (USA)

If someone goes to the forest and dies there, he would die alone. That would be sad for him. I would not like that. When I die, I want to be at home with my family with everyone paying attention to me.
Endriyas, age 13 (Ethiopia)

If I do good things in my lifetime, then I will not mind dying. I believe in life after death. I want to complete my ideas and intentions, and after that, it is okay if I die.
Fitsum, age 16 (Ethiopia)

I remember my father's death. My father suffered for seven years before he died. I don't want anyone to have to go through that. *Nuredin, age 13 (Ethiopia)*

I never want anyone to die before they have accomplished their life's purpose. Also, I don't want to be buried in the ground. It scares me. *Kidist, age 13 (Ethiopia)*

A mom may have only one child. She would imagine her child having wonderful dreams and doing so many things. If death comes early, it would make the mom very sad that her child would not be able to live out her dreams.
Tigist, age 9 (Ethiopia)

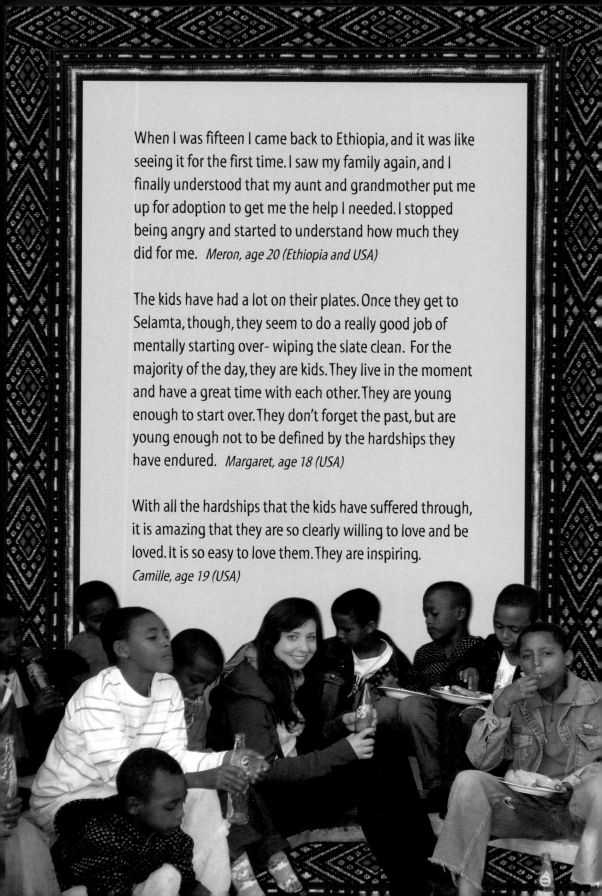

When I was fifteen I came back to Ethiopia, and it was like seeing it for the first time. I saw my family again, and I finally understood that my aunt and grandmother put me up for adoption to get me the help I needed. I stopped being angry and started to understand how much they did for me. *Meron, age 20 (Ethiopia and USA)*

The kids have had a lot on their plates. Once they get to Selamta, though, they seem to do a really good job of mentally starting over- wiping the slate clean. For the majority of the day, they are kids. They live in the moment and have a great time with each other. They are young enough to start over. They don't forget the past, but are young enough not to be defined by the hardships they have endured. *Margaret, age 18 (USA)*

With all the hardships that the kids have suffered through, it is amazing that they are so clearly willing to love and be loved. It is so easy to love them. They are inspiring.
Camille, age 19 (USA)

For me, there was just happiness when I came to Selamta,
not sadness. *Ermiyas, age 12 (Ethiopia)*

When someone loves you, like "Mom," it changes your life.
I know that she loves me because she is changing my life.
Fitsum, age 16 (Ethiopia)

The main thing that I get from my family here is love. Also,
everything is done for me. I just have to help. I get to be a
kid, and don't have to worry about getting food and
finding a place to sleep. *Dawit, age 8 (Ethiopia)*

When someone tries to share my ides, whether they are
good things or bad things, just the sharing makes me feel
happy. *Kidist, age 13 (Ethiopia)*

When I cry and someone holds me, I feel loved. When I
need help, and someone helps me, I feel loved.
Hailu, age 7 (Ethiopia)

For me, a friend is someone who keeps my secrets and helps me when I am in trouble.
Mekedes, age 14 (Ethiopia)

One afternoon, Meron and I were putting together a present for Teddy. We asked Robel, Teddy's closest friend, what Teddy needed. Knowing how much Teddy loved soccer, and that he did not own any proper shoes to play in, Robel eagerly told us that Teddy would love a pair of cleats. Meron and I found a new pair of cleats, and Robel helped us to wrap them up nicely. As we watched Teddy unwrap his gift, I noticed Robel had tears in his eyes. Robel was happier to see his closest friend get cleats than he would have been to get them himself. This was touching and another example of how close the Selamta family is.
Zoe, age 21 (USA)

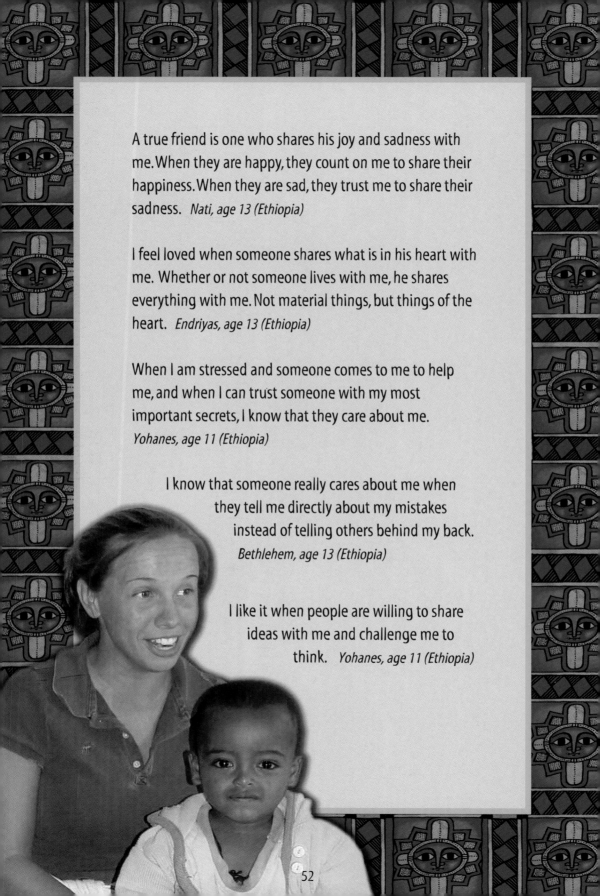

A true friend is one who shares his joy and sadness with me. When they are happy, they count on me to share their happiness. When they are sad, they trust me to share their sadness. *Nati, age 13 (Ethiopia)*

I feel loved when someone shares what is in his heart with me. Whether or not someone lives with me, he shares everything with me. Not material things, but things of the heart. *Endriyas, age 13 (Ethiopia)*

When I am stressed and someone comes to me to help me, and when I can trust someone with my most important secrets, I know that they care about me. *Yohanes, age 11 (Ethiopia)*

I know that someone really cares about me when they tell me directly about my mistakes instead of telling others behind my back. *Bethlehem, age 13 (Ethiopia)*

I like it when people are willing to share ideas with me and challenge me to think. *Yohanes, age 11 (Ethiopia)*

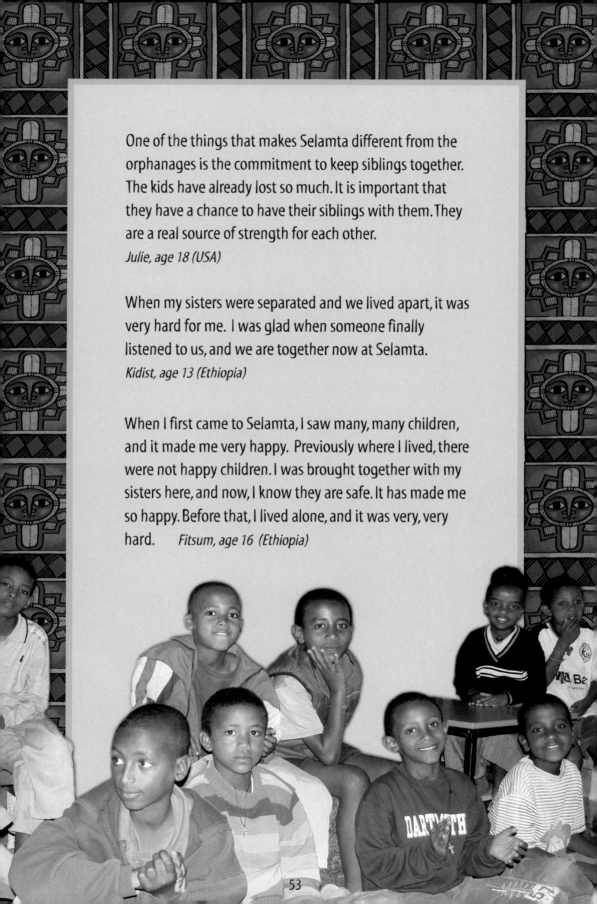

One of the things that makes Selamta different from the orphanages is the commitment to keep siblings together. The kids have already lost so much. It is important that they have a chance to have their siblings with them. They are a real source of strength for each other.
Julie, age 18 (USA)

When my sisters were separated and we lived apart, it was very hard for me. I was glad when someone finally listened to us, and we are together now at Selamta.
Kidist, age 13 (Ethiopia)

When I first came to Selamta, I saw many, many children, and it made me very happy. Previously where I lived, there were not happy children. I was brought together with my sisters here, and now, I know they are safe. It has made me so happy. Before that, I lived alone, and it was very, very hard.   *Fitsum, age 16 (Ethiopia)*

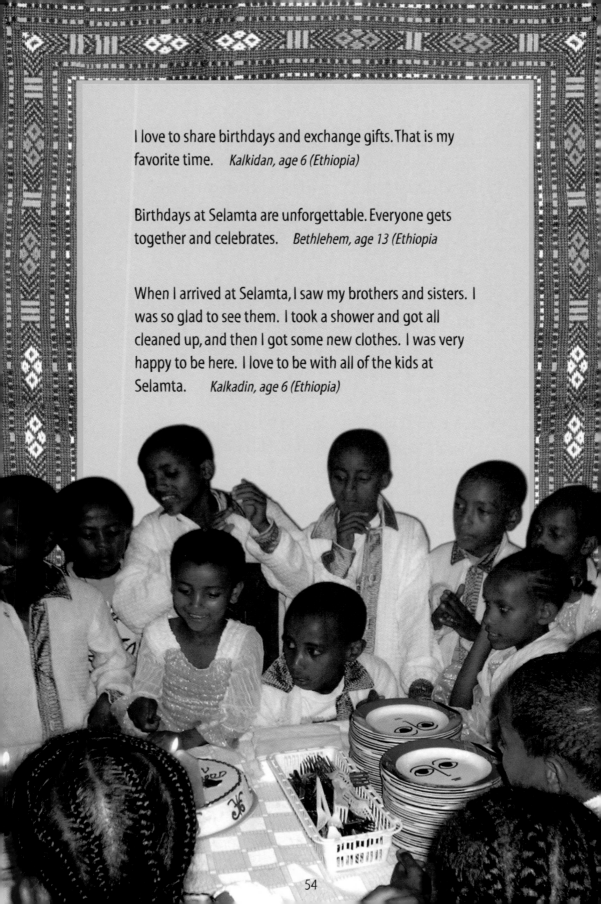

I love to share birthdays and exchange gifts. That is my favorite time. *Kalkidan, age 6 (Ethiopia)*

Birthdays at Selamta are unforgettable. Everyone gets together and celebrates. *Bethlehem, age 13 (Ethiopia*

When I arrived at Selamta, I saw my brothers and sisters. I was so glad to see them. I took a shower and got all cleaned up, and then I got some new clothes. I was very happy to be here. I love to be with all of the kids at Selamta. *Kalkadin, age 6 (Ethiopia)*

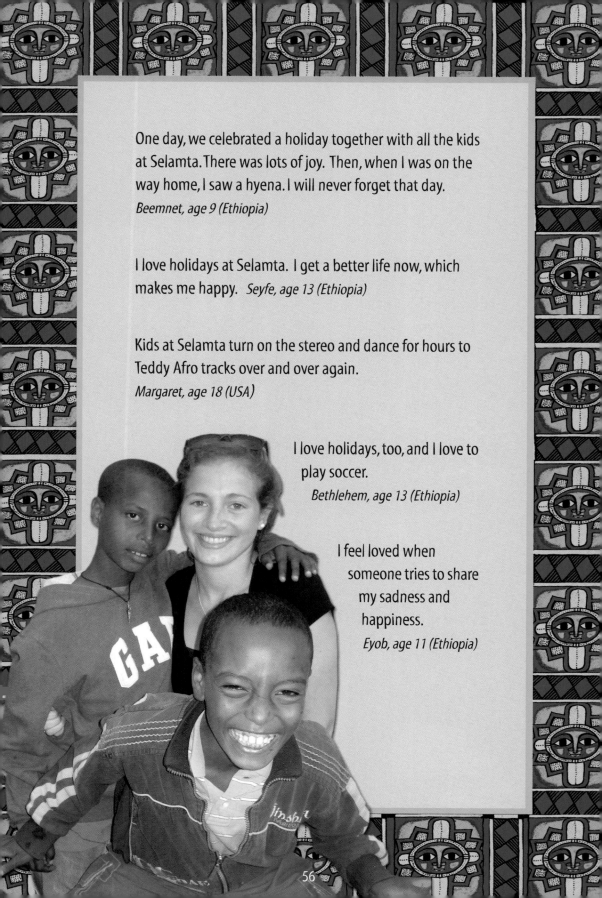

One day, we celebrated a holiday together with all the kids at Selamta. There was lots of joy. Then, when I was on the way home, I saw a hyena. I will never forget that day.
Beemnet, age 9 (Ethiopia)

I love holidays at Selamta. I get a better life now, which makes me happy. *Seyfe, age 13 (Ethiopia)*

Kids at Selamta turn on the stereo and dance for hours to Teddy Afro tracks over and over again.
Margaret, age 18 (USA)

I love holidays, too, and I love to play soccer.
Bethlehem, age 13 (Ethiopia)

I feel loved when someone tries to share my sadness and happiness.
Eyob, age 11 (Ethiopia)

The kids find so much happiness in each other and share it with those of us who come from America to be with them. Every morning they welcome us with a hug and a kiss. They find joy in the smallest things. A little rubber ball can provide entertainment for hours. They create their own fun through being with each other. With one soccer ball, even the little guys are allowed to play alongside the very talented older kids. Everyone is included and everyone has a good time. *Margaret, age 18 (USA)*

When someone loves me, he is sharing my ideas. When I feel sad or happy, someone shares these things, and I feel loved. *Belay, age 16 (Ethiopia)*

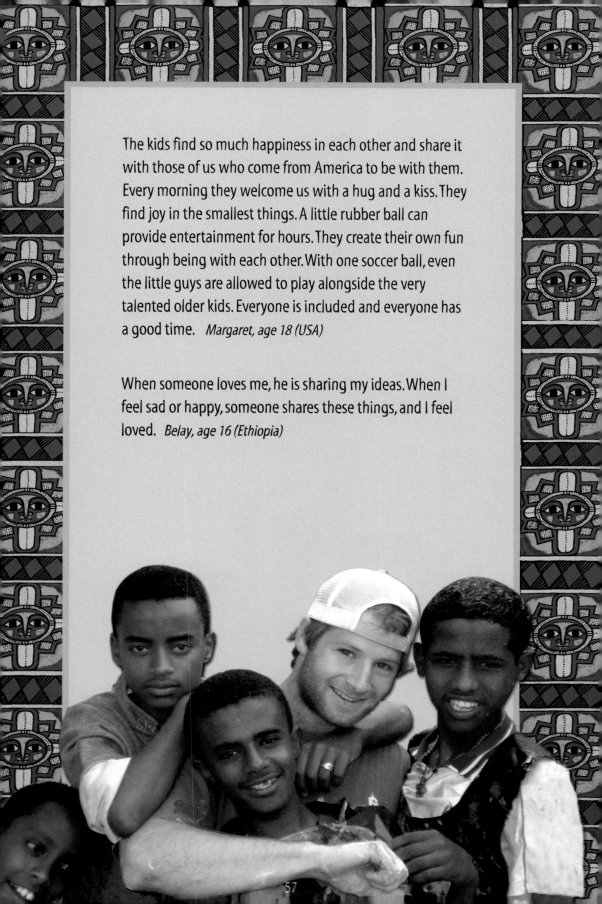

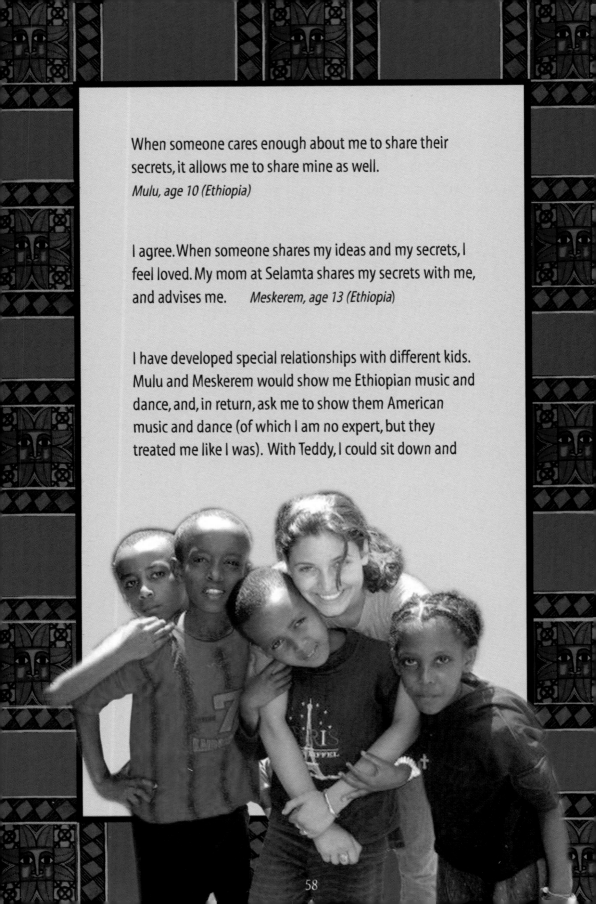

When someone cares enough about me to share their
secrets, it allows me to share mine as well.
Mulu, age 10 (Ethiopia)

I agree. When someone shares my ideas and my secrets, I
feel loved. My mom at Selamta shares my secrets with me,
and advises me.   *Meskerem, age 13 (Ethiopia)*

I have developed special relationships with different kids.
Mulu and Meskerem would show me Ethiopian music and
dance, and, in return, ask me to show them American
music and dance (of which I am no expert, but they
treated me like I was). With Teddy, I could sit down and

have a meaningful conversation, and with Mariyamawit, I was always up for a snuggle and a nap.

Robyn, age 21 (USA)

One thing that is really important to me is to be able to go to church services. Church is important to me, and before I was at Selamta, there was no way for me to go to church. At Selamta, we are allowed to follow our hearts and pray in the way that we believe. *Sentayehu age 13 (Ethiopia)*

My friend, Salam, is the same age as I am, and she shares everything with me. She is a great example of love.

Miheret, age 8 (Ethiopia)

I share my secrets with Miheret, too.

Selam, age 7 (Ethiopia)

I loved spending time with Seyfe. He couldn't go to school because of the problems that he has had with his eyes, so he worked with me on a mapping project to create a map of the neighborhood. He has a huge heart.

Seyfe is a really good soccer player, but can't play in the games because of his eyes. When there was a soccer game, Seyfe got all the fans together and led cheers for his friends. There was no one with more spirit in the place.

John, age 21 (USA)

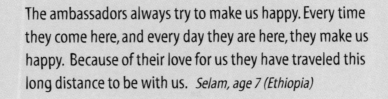

The ambassadors always try to make us happy. Every time they come here, and every day they are here, they make us happy. Because of their love for us they have traveled this long distance to be with us. *Selam, age 7 (Ethiopia)*

I will never forget the day that I got my sponsor. That was the happiest day for me. *Nuredin, age 13 (Ethiopia)*

I consider all of the kids part of my family, but there is a special relationship with the kids we sponsor. When I first came into Selamta, I noticed that Eyob was looking at me and watching me with an expectant look on his face. As he continued to watch me, I went up to talk with him. He looked up at me showed me a crinkled up picture of my mother and me that he had been keeping with him. It was so sweet. *Julie, age 18 (USA)*

Before I went to Ethiopia, I studied a collection of pictures of the children our family sponsors in hopes that I could recognize them upon my arrival. Three boys, just like my family in America. They looked adorable in the pictures; it was hard to believe that they were fending for themselves on the city streets not too long before. When Carol showed the photos to us, she explained how Temesgen, the four-year-old youngest brother, had an entire side of his face swollen up when he got to Selamta because of the gutter water he had been drinking to survive. This was the first time I realized how much the kids need our help.

Christopher, age 18 (USA)

After two months spending every day with the kids at Selamta, I recognized that we had become family. I was amazed that, despite the language barrier, I had made real and lasting friendships with the children. Everyone was so caring and spirited. When I first imagined Ethiopia, I thought only of what I could do to help the people there. By the time I had to leave, I realized how much I had gained from their influence. The Ethiopian people taught me about joy and respect - values that are of the utmost importance in their culture.   *Ben, age 21 (USA)*

I am very thankful because of my life now.
Bilal, age 10 (Ethiopia)

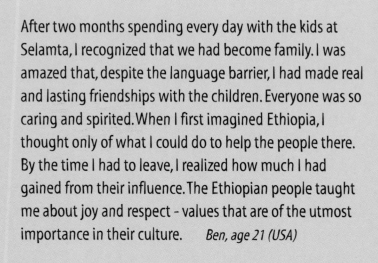

I like Selamta because before I was here, I had a very bad life, and now I have a very, very happy life. The children at Selamta are beautiful, and I love the ambassadors because they each give a different gift. *Robel, 15 (Ethiopia)*

I like playing with all the kids.
Chernet, age 7 (Ethiopia)

Selamta is really about family. Other orphanages provide housing for kids, but not necessarily family. Selamta's small houses create new families; it is ingrained in them.

Alexandra, age 18 (USA)

The language barrier just isn't that much of an issue. Everyone is at Selamta for the same purpose. When the kids are excited about something it is contagious and you join in. Also, you learn to be attentive to non-verbal cues like fatigue. When you respond, they respond. It just works.

Johnny, age 20 (USA)

This summer I am very happy because we went on a trip to Sodere to swim.

Abel, age 12 (Ethiopia)

I love it when all the kids are together.

Tizita, age 9 (Ethiopia)

I really like the times that we go on special trips with the people I love from Selamta. Once we took a photo, and whenever I see the photo, I remember how much I loved it.

Mekedes, age 14 (Ethiopia)

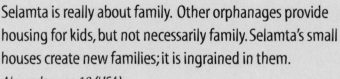

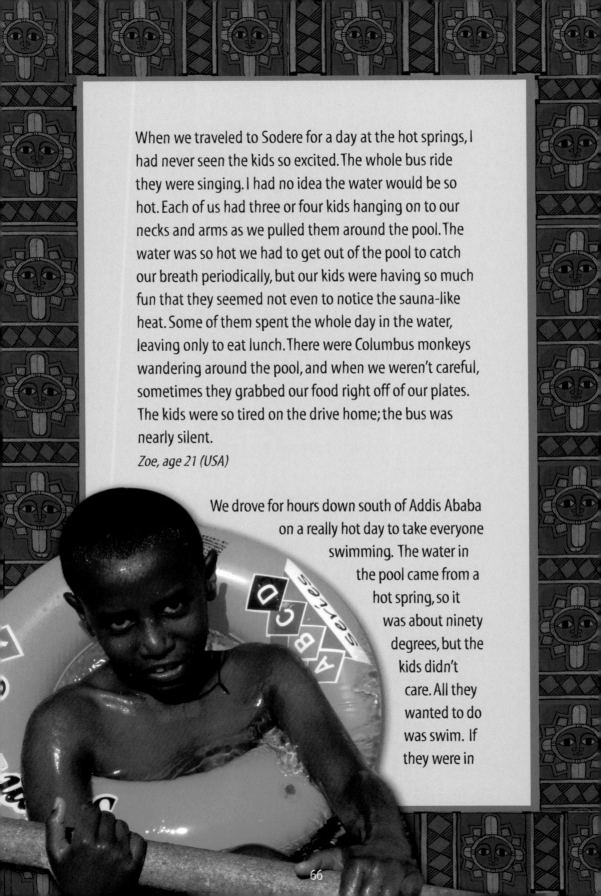

When we traveled to Sodere for a day at the hot springs, I had never seen the kids so excited. The whole bus ride they were singing. I had no idea the water would be so hot. Each of us had three or four kids hanging on to our necks and arms as we pulled them around the pool. The water was so hot we had to get out of the pool to catch our breath periodically, but our kids were having so much fun that they seemed not even to notice the sauna-like heat. Some of them spent the whole day in the water, leaving only to eat lunch. There were Columbus monkeys wandering around the pool, and when we weren't careful, sometimes they grabbed our food right off of our plates. The kids were so tired on the drive home; the bus was nearly silent.

Zoe, age 21 (USA)

We drove for hours down south of Addis Ababa on a really hot day to take everyone swimming. The water in the pool came from a hot spring, so it was about ninety degrees, but the kids didn't care. All they wanted to do was swim. If they were in

the water, we were in the water. We each had two and four kids hanging on our arms every minute. The kids were in heaven.   *Meron, age 20 (Ethiopia and USA)*

We visited Sodere this summer. In Sodere, they have fresh air, a pool and wild animals. They have a beautiful hotel and a wash river. People should come to visit Ethiopia to see Sodere.   *Nati, age 13 (Ethiopia)*

I love Selamta. My family is the best family because my mother and auntie at Selamta are very fine. Selamta is my gift of love. I have shoes, good food and a good school. And also, I love my brothers and sisters.   *Abel, age 12 (Ethiopia)*

The moms and aunties bring all of Selamta together. Their loving and caring attitude, and their attentive care of the kids, makes each home at Selamta feel like a family.   *Ben, age 21 (USA)*

The kids are all involved in doing chores to help with the care of their homes. They all make their beds, sweep their houses, fold their clothes and help with everything. They work all together, and they take turns doing dishes and chores. Even the little ones help. That is just what families do.   *Meron, age 20 (USA)*

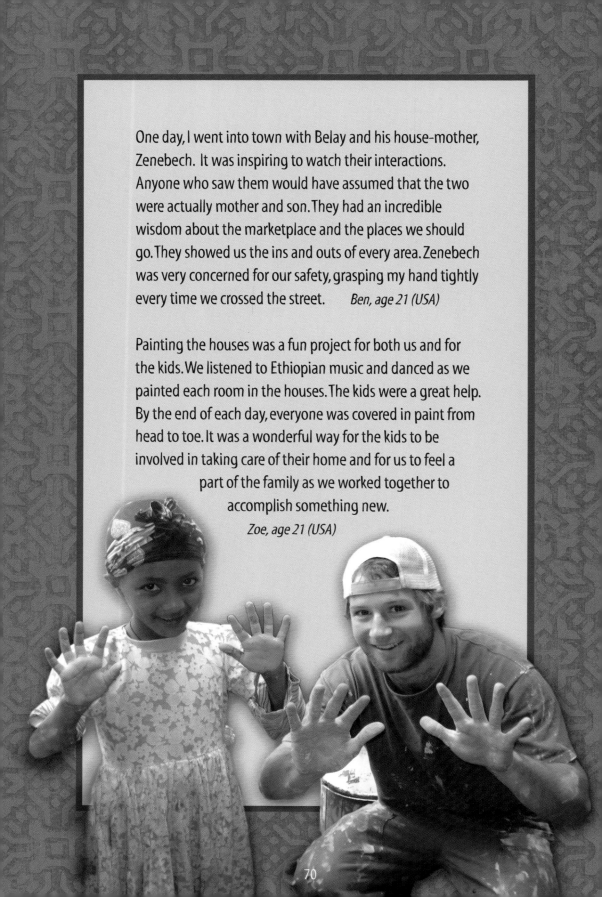

One day, I went into town with Belay and his house-mother, Zenebech. It was inspiring to watch their interactions. Anyone who saw them would have assumed that the two were actually mother and son. They had an incredible wisdom about the marketplace and the places we should go. They showed us the ins and outs of every area. Zenebech was very concerned for our safety, grasping my hand tightly every time we crossed the street.   *Ben, age 21 (USA)*

Painting the houses was a fun project for both us and for the kids. We listened to Ethiopian music and danced as we painted each room in the houses. The kids were a great help. By the end of each day, everyone was covered in paint from head to toe. It was a wonderful way for the kids to be involved in taking care of their home and for us to feel a part of the family as we worked together to accomplish something new.

Zoe, age 21 (USA)

We created painting crews to paint the houses where each new family lived. The crews included the American kids and the older Ethiopian kids. We would bring out a bucket of paint, listen to Teddy Afro music turned up loud, and we'd paint like crazy. All the younger kids wanted to be a part of helping any way they could. They would come in with their work clothes on, and their hair tied up. They looked at us with the paintbrushes and said, "Can I try, can I try?" Even the youngest kids would grab their rags and clean up any paint that got on the floor. In the end, their houses were beautiful, and they had had a part in it. They were proud to be a part of the work crew.   *Meron, age 20 (Ethiopia and USA)*

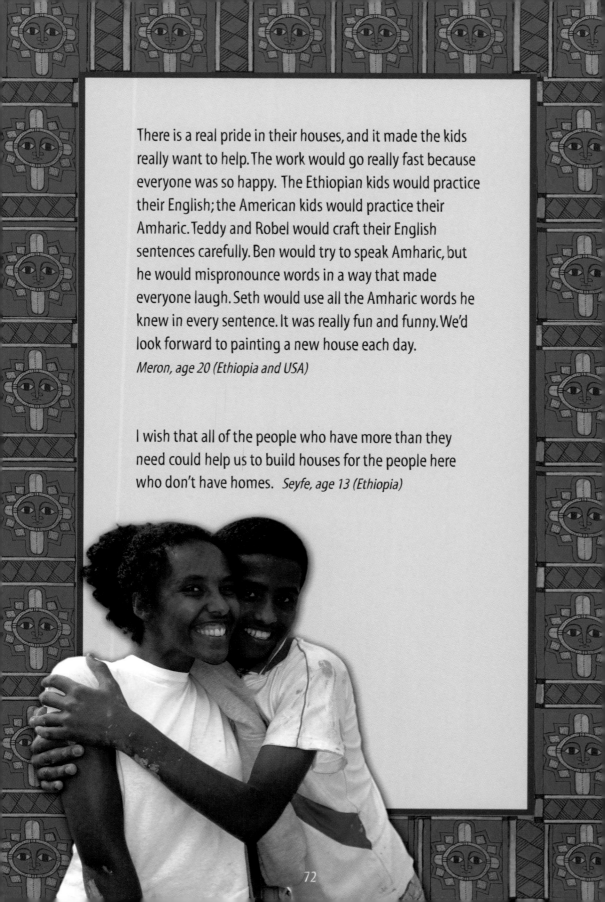

There is a real pride in their houses, and it made the kids really want to help. The work would go really fast because everyone was so happy. The Ethiopian kids would practice their English; the American kids would practice their Amharic. Teddy and Robel would craft their English sentences carefully. Ben would try to speak Amharic, but he would mispronounce words in a way that made everyone laugh. Seth would use all the Amharic words he knew in every sentence. It was really fun and funny. We'd look forward to painting a new house each day.
Meron, age 20 (Ethiopia and USA)

I wish that all of the people who have more than they need could help us to build houses for the people here who don't have homes. *Seyfe, age 13 (Ethiopia)*

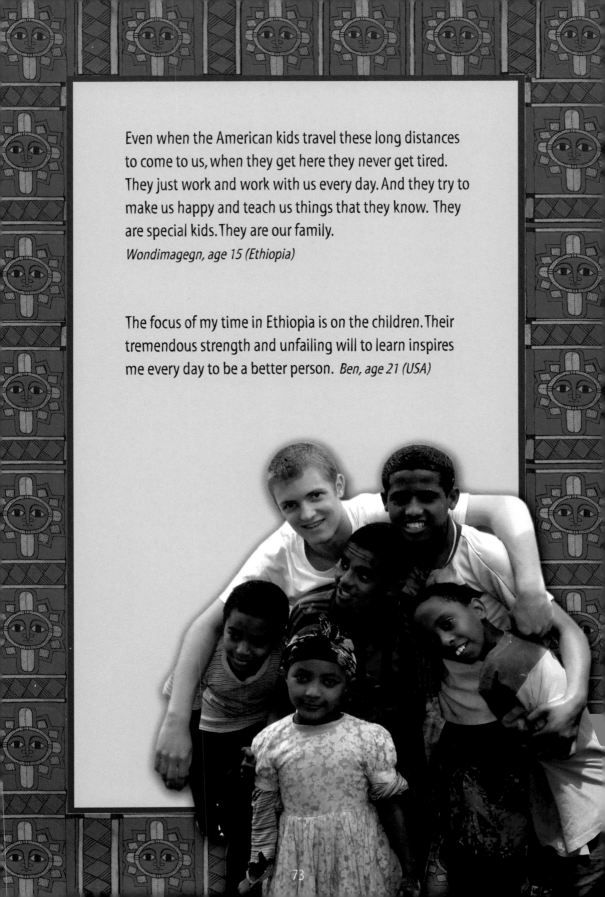

Even when the American kids travel these long distances to come to us, when they get here they never get tired. They just work and work with us every day. And they try to make us happy and teach us things that they know. They are special kids. They are our family.

Wondimagegn, age 15 (Ethiopia)

The focus of my time in Ethiopia is on the children. Their tremendous strength and unfailing will to learn inspires me every day to be a better person. *Ben, age 21 (USA)*

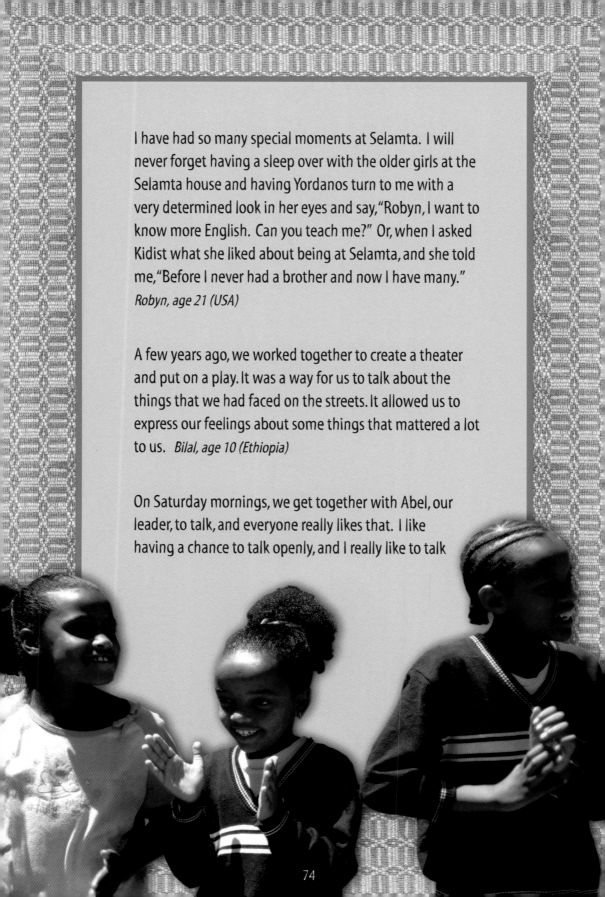

I have had so many special moments at Selamta. I will never forget having a sleep over with the older girls at the Selamta house and having Yordanos turn to me with a very determined look in her eyes and say, "Robyn, I want to know more English. Can you teach me?" Or, when I asked Kidist what she liked about being at Selamta, and she told me, "Before I never had a brother and now I have many."
Robyn, age 21 (USA)

A few years ago, we worked together to create a theater and put on a play. It was a way for us to talk about the things that we had faced on the streets. It allowed us to express our feelings about some things that mattered a lot to us. *Bilal, age 10 (Ethiopia)*

On Saturday mornings, we get together with Abel, our leader, to talk, and everyone really likes that. I like having a chance to talk openly, and I really like to talk

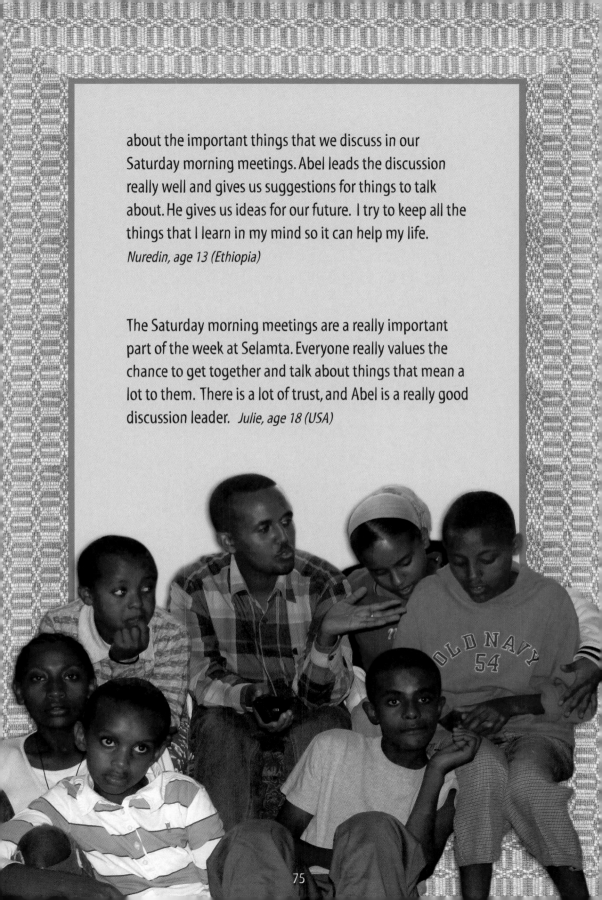

about the important things that we discuss in our Saturday morning meetings. Abel leads the discussion really well and gives us suggestions for things to talk about. He gives us ideas for our future. I try to keep all the things that I learn in my mind so it can help my life.
Nuredin, age 13 (Ethiopia)

The Saturday morning meetings are a really important part of the week at Selamta. Everyone really values the chance to get together and talk about things that mean a lot to them. There is a lot of trust, and Abel is a really good discussion leader. *Julie, age 18 (USA)*

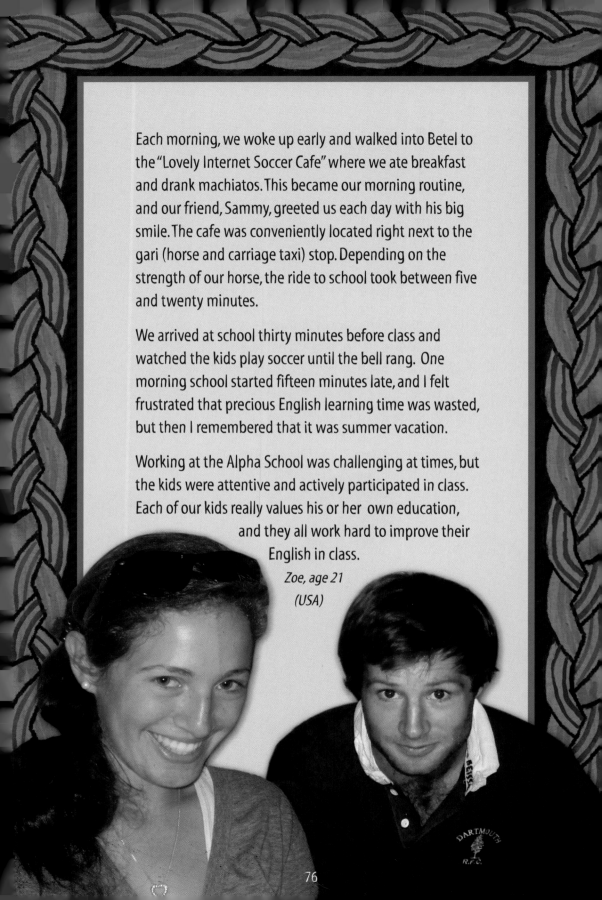

Each morning, we woke up early and walked into Betel to the "Lovely Internet Soccer Cafe" where we ate breakfast and drank machiatos. This became our morning routine, and our friend, Sammy, greeted us each day with his big smile. The cafe was conveniently located right next to the gari (horse and carriage taxi) stop. Depending on the strength of our horse, the ride to school took between five and twenty minutes.

We arrived at school thirty minutes before class and watched the kids play soccer until the bell rang. One morning school started fifteen minutes late, and I felt frustrated that precious English learning time was wasted, but then I remembered that it was summer vacation.

Working at the Alpha School was challenging at times, but the kids were attentive and actively participated in class. Each of our kids really values his or her own education, and they all work hard to improve their English in class.

Zoe, age 21
(USA)

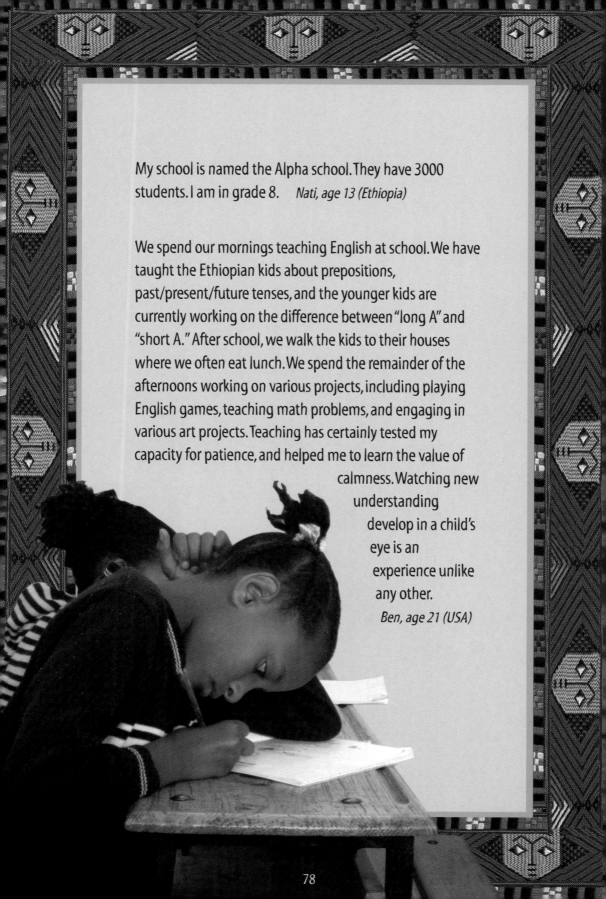

My school is named the Alpha school. They have 3000 students. I am in grade 8.   *Nati, age 13 (Ethiopia)*

We spend our mornings teaching English at school. We have taught the Ethiopian kids about prepositions, past/present/future tenses, and the younger kids are currently working on the difference between "long A" and "short A." After school, we walk the kids to their houses where we often eat lunch. We spend the remainder of the afternoons working on various projects, including playing English games, teaching math problems, and engaging in various art projects. Teaching has certainly tested my capacity for patience, and helped me to learn the value of calmness. Watching new understanding develop in a child's eye is an experience unlike any other.

Ben, age 21 (USA)

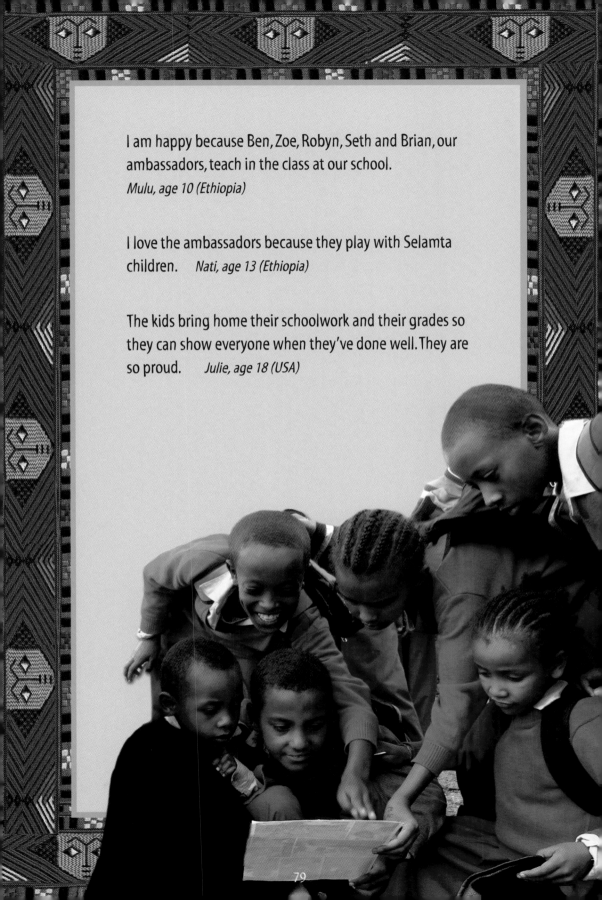

I am happy because Ben, Zoe, Robyn, Seth and Brian, our ambassadors, teach in the class at our school.
Mulu, age 10 (Ethiopia)

I love the ambassadors because they play with Selamta children. *Nati, age 13 (Ethiopia)*

The kids bring home their schoolwork and their grades so they can show everyone when they've done well. They are so proud. *Julie, age 18 (USA)*

79

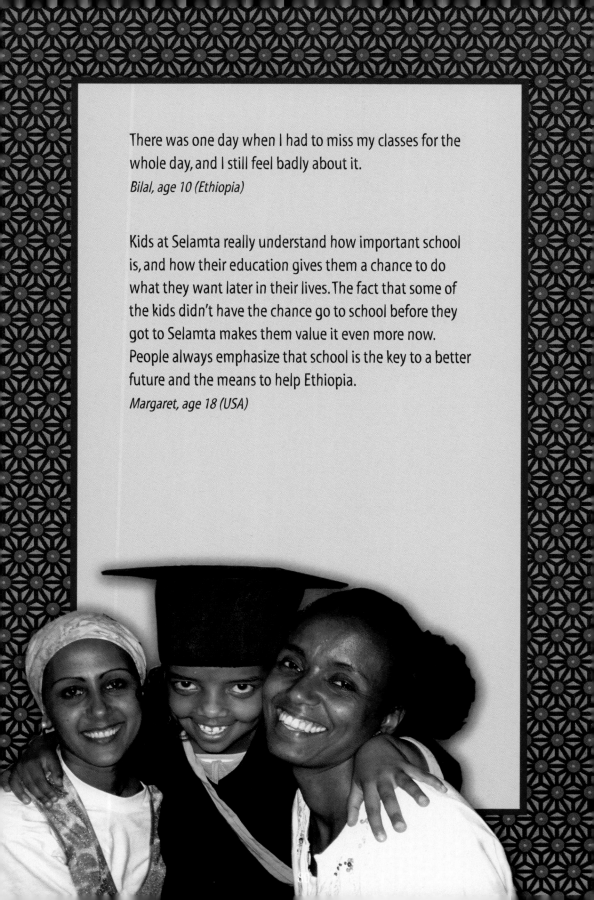

There was one day when I had to miss my classes for the whole day, and I still feel badly about it.
Bilal, age 10 (Ethiopia)

Kids at Selamta really understand how important school is, and how their education gives them a chance to do what they want later in their lives. The fact that some of the kids didn't have the chance go to school before they got to Selamta makes them value it even more now. People always emphasize that school is the key to a better future and the means to help Ethiopia.
Margaret, age 18 (USA)

What I love most at Selamta is meeting all the kids when they come out of school. I love the warm greetings and recognition. Even when we have been away for a while, they know exactly who we are right away and run up and give us hugs. It is amazing to see how much Selamta has grown, and how much the kids have grown in the two years that I was away. *Alexandra, age 18 (USA)*

We had a ceremony for the kids who were at the top of their classes in school, and gifts were given. These kids were able to stand up in front of their brothers and sisters and show how hard they had worked. For some of them, it was the first time in their lives they had been singled out and rewarded for their hard work. The looks on their faces showed how proud they were to have done so well in school. *Margaret, age 18 (USA)*

I am happiest when I am playing soccer.
Yohanes, age 11 (Ethiopia)

Especially when the soccer coach is working with us.
Temesgen, age 6 (Ethiopia)

Whenever we could, we would play futball (soccer) with
the kids. It was great, because they just played for fun. Flat
out. They had an uneven field, mostly dirt, and two
goalposts made from sticks, but they had the time of their
lives. Everyone was allowed to play, and smiles never left
their faces during the time they were on the field.
Ben, age 21 (USA)

I will never forget the day we got the trophy for winning
the soccer game.   *Eyob, age 11 (Ethiopia)*

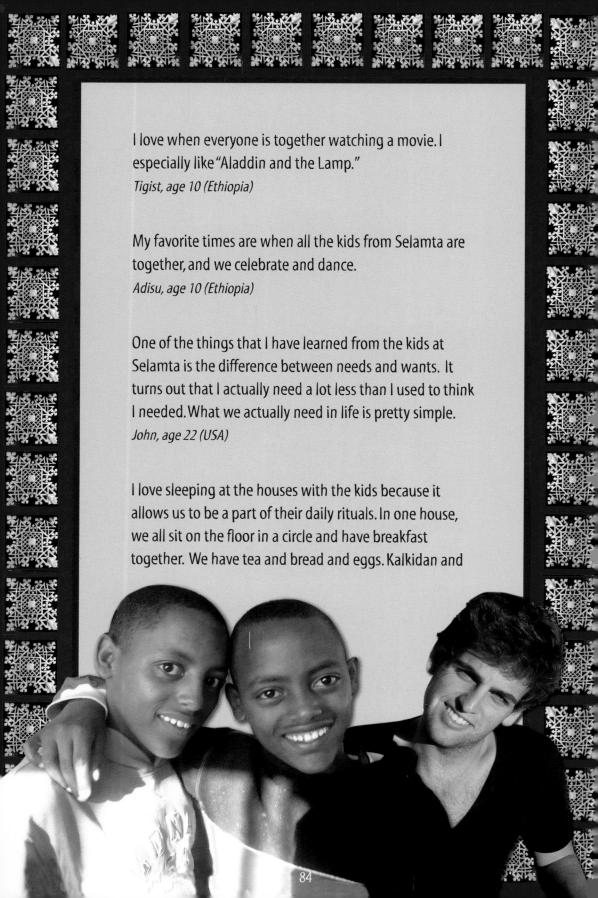

I love when everyone is together watching a movie. I especially like "Aladdin and the Lamp."
Tigist, age 10 (Ethiopia)

My favorite times are when all the kids from Selamta are together, and we celebrate and dance.
Adisu, age 10 (Ethiopia)

One of the things that I have learned from the kids at Selamta is the difference between needs and wants. It turns out that I actually need a lot less than I used to think I needed. What we actually need in life is pretty simple.
John, age 22 (USA)

I love sleeping at the houses with the kids because it allows us to be a part of their daily rituals. In one house, we all sit on the floor in a circle and have breakfast together. We have tea and bread and eggs. Kalkidan and

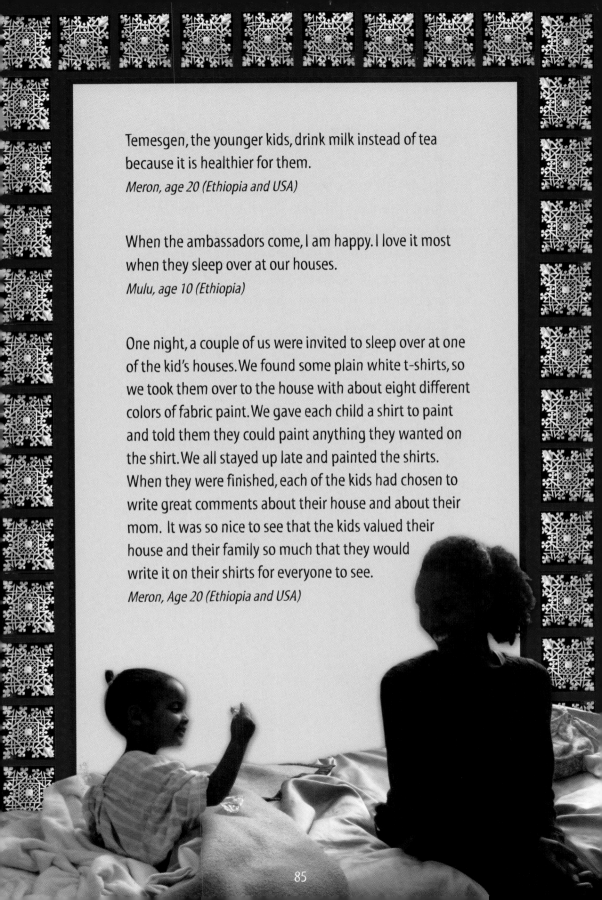

Temesgen, the younger kids, drink milk instead of tea because it is healthier for them.

Meron, age 20 (Ethiopia and USA)

When the ambassadors come, I am happy. I love it most when they sleep over at our houses.

Mulu, age 10 (Ethiopia)

One night, a couple of us were invited to sleep over at one of the kid's houses. We found some plain white t-shirts, so we took them over to the house with about eight different colors of fabric paint. We gave each child a shirt to paint and told them they could paint anything they wanted on the shirt. We all stayed up late and painted the shirts. When they were finished, each of the kids had chosen to write great comments about their house and about their mom. It was so nice to see that the kids valued their house and their family so much that they would write it on their shirts for everyone to see.

Meron, Age 20 (Ethiopia and USA)

Shortly before I had to leave Selamta to return to the USA, Robel, Teddy, Nati and Wendimagegn asked me to take them to see the soccer game. I took them to the game as I had done before, but this time, they brought their own money and paid for themselves. On the way back, they stopped. I asked them why they were stopping, and they pulled out notes they had written to me. In the notes, they told me that they considered me to be their sister.

Alexandra, age 18 (USA)

We have Selmata Idol night where everyone performs songs and skits. It is one of everyone's favorite events. One night, when little Temesgen was going to perform, he stood up in front of the group ready to start his act. After he stood up, he suddenly remembered that had just lost his front tooth. He was so embarrassed that he put his hand in front of his mouth and couldn't sing. He didn't realize that his missing tooth made him even cuter than he already was.

Meron, age 20 (Ethiopia and USA)

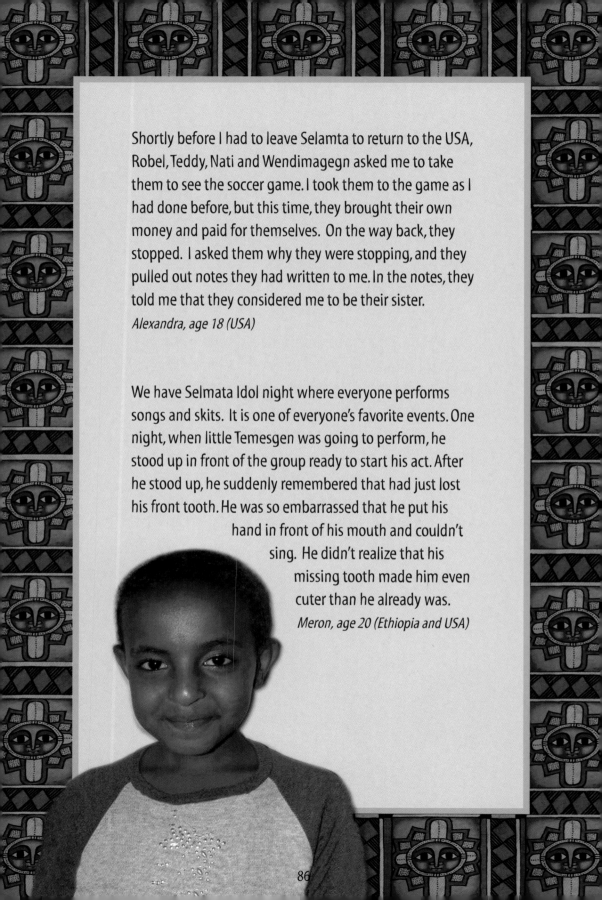

I know that Ethiopia is a developing country. I want it to develop in a positive and constructive way. Everyone here knows about the United States. I would like everyone to know about Ethiopia in a positive way.
Mekedes, age 14 (Ethiopia)

My vision of the future is to have everyone working side by side to help each other, instead of leaving some people aside. I want to see everyone helping each other in good and bad times. That is the way we are going to eradicate poverty and disease. *Nati, age 13 (Ethiopia)*

There are many very special things about Ethiopia. If other people in the world knew more about us, they would know of some of the things that we do well. Maybe they could try some of these things. *Beemnet, age 9 (Ethiopia)*

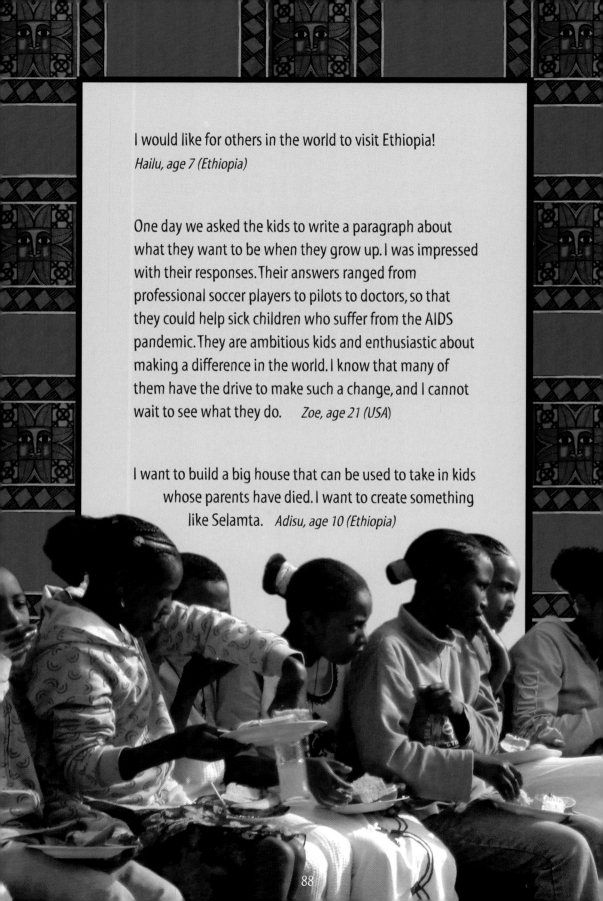

I would like for others in the world to visit Ethiopia!
Hailu, age 7 (Ethiopia)

One day we asked the kids to write a paragraph about what they want to be when they grow up. I was impressed with their responses. Their answers ranged from professional soccer players to pilots to doctors, so that they could help sick children who suffer from the AIDS pandemic. They are ambitious kids and enthusiastic about making a difference in the world. I know that many of them have the drive to make such a change, and I cannot wait to see what they do.   *Zoe, age 21 (USA)*

I want to build a big house that can be used to take in kids whose parents have died. I want to create something like Selamta.   *Adisu, age 10 (Ethiopia)*

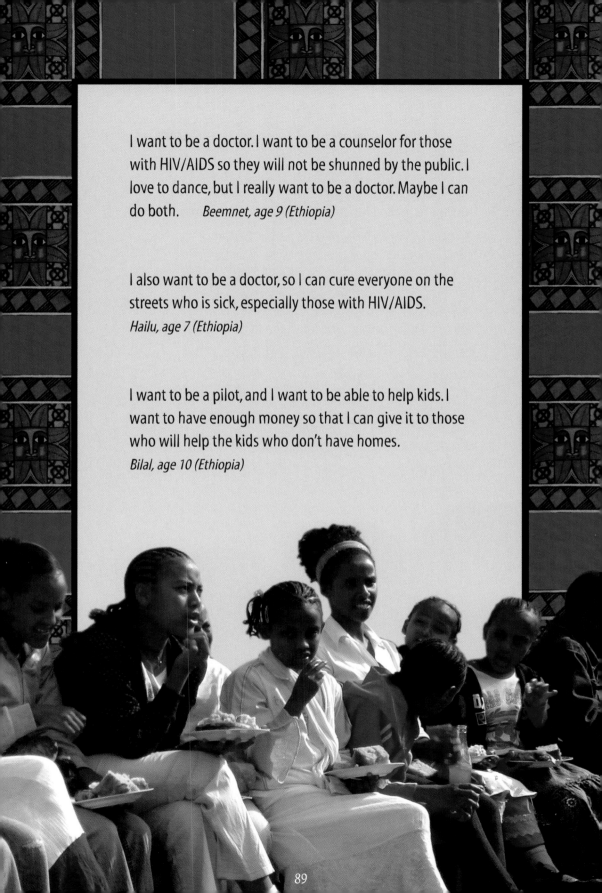

I want to be a doctor. I want to be a counselor for those with HIV/AIDS so they will not be shunned by the public. I love to dance, but I really want to be a doctor. Maybe I can do both.   *Beemnet, age 9 (Ethiopia)*

I also want to be a doctor, so I can cure everyone on the streets who is sick, especially those with HIV/AIDS.
Hailu, age 7 (Ethiopia)

I want to be a pilot, and I want to be able to help kids. I want to have enough money so that I can give it to those who will help the kids who don't have homes.
Bilal, age 10 (Ethiopia)

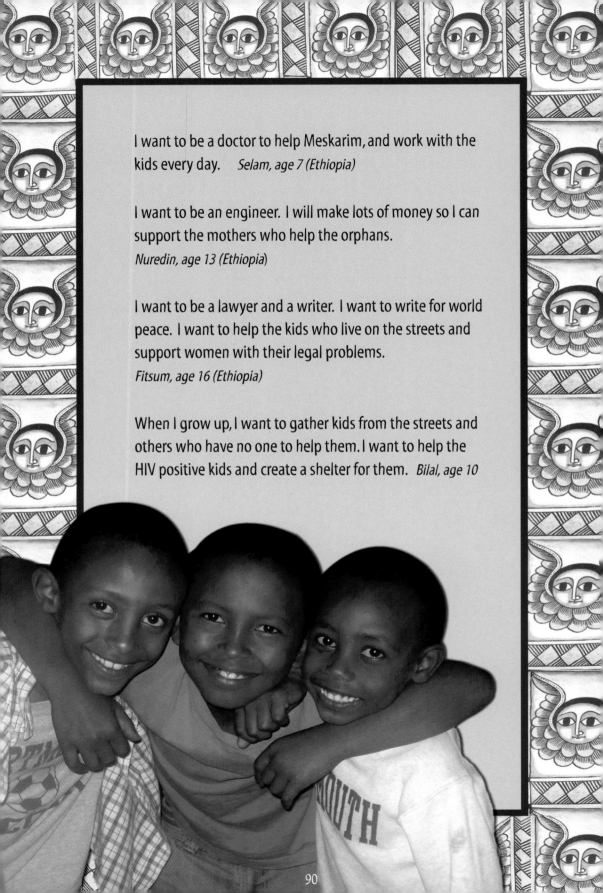

I want to be a doctor to help Meskarim, and work with the kids every day. *Selam, age 7 (Ethiopia)*

I want to be an engineer. I will make lots of money so I can support the mothers who help the orphans.
Nuredin, age 13 (Ethiopia)

I want to be a lawyer and a writer. I want to write for world peace. I want to help the kids who live on the streets and support women with their legal problems.
Fitsum, age 16 (Ethiopia)

When I grow up, I want to gather kids from the streets and others who have no one to help them. I want to help the HIV positive kids and create a shelter for them. *Bilal, age 10*

I want to be a scientist, and I want to work with Bethlehem. *Endriyas, age 13 (Ethiopia)*

I want to be a pilot so I can fly to different parts of the world. *Yohanes, age 11 (Ethiopia)*

First, I would like to get medication for my eye. Then, I would like to help the kind woman who helped bring me to Selamta. Sometimes, she comes to visit me here. *Seyfe, age 13 (Ethiopia)*

When I am big, I want to drive a car.
Where would you drive your car?
Forward.
Temesgen, age 6
(Ethiopia)

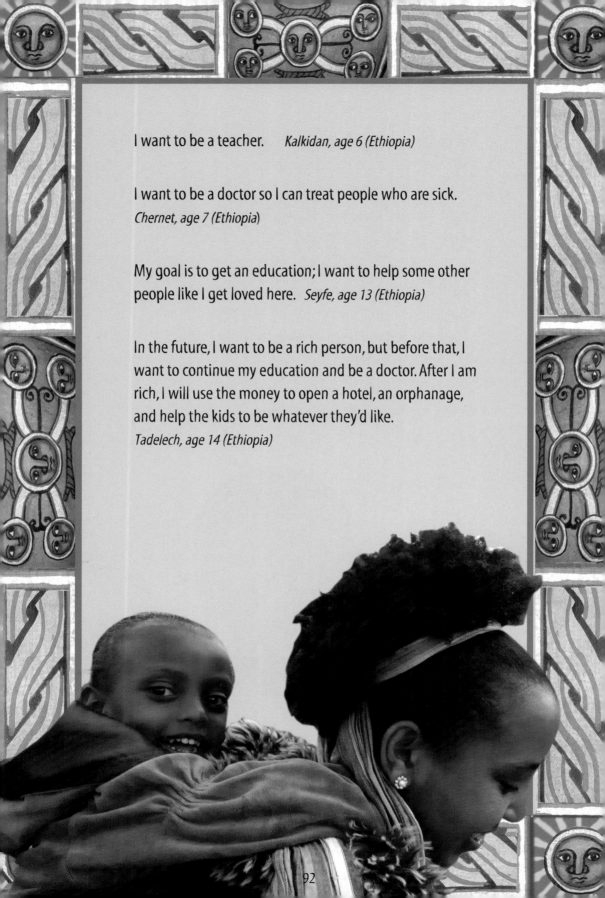

I want to be a teacher.   *Kalkidan, age 6 (Ethiopia)*

I want to be a doctor so I can treat people who are sick.
Chernet, age 7 (Ethiopia)

My goal is to get an education; I want to help some other people like I get loved here. *Seyfe, age 13 (Ethiopia)*

In the future, I want to be a rich person, but before that, I want to continue my education and be a doctor. After I am rich, I will use the money to open a hotel, an orphanage, and help the kids to be whatever they'd like.
Tadelech, age 14 (Ethiopia)

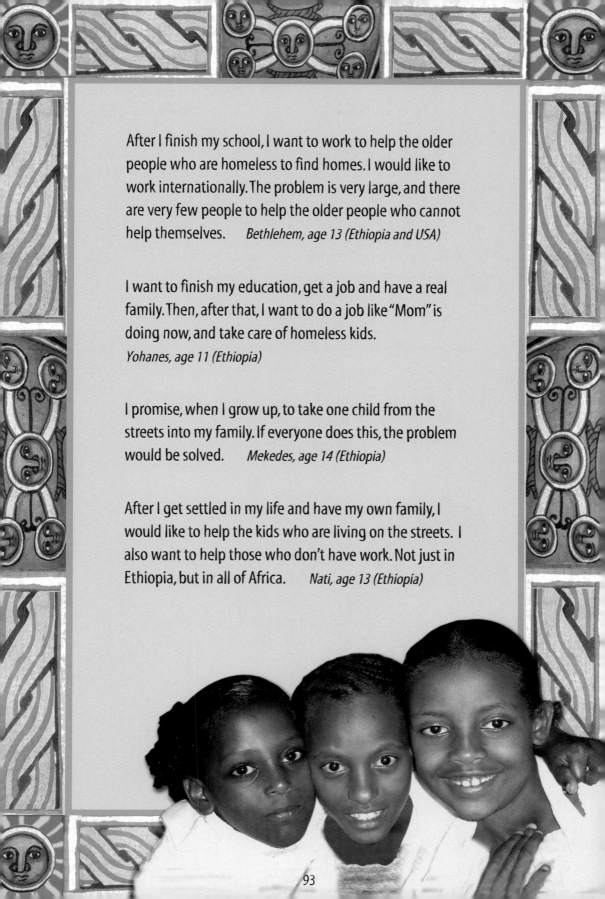

After I finish my school, I want to work to help the older people who are homeless to find homes. I would like to work internationally. The problem is very large, and there are very few people to help the older people who cannot help themselves.   *Bethlehem, age 13 (Ethiopia and USA)*

I want to finish my education, get a job and have a real family. Then, after that, I want to do a job like "Mom" is doing now, and take care of homeless kids.
Yohanes, age 11 (Ethiopia)

I promise, when I grow up, to take one child from the streets into my family. If everyone does this, the problem would be solved.   *Mekedes, age 14 (Ethiopia)*

After I get settled in my life and have my own family, I would like to help the kids who are living on the streets. I also want to help those who don't have work. Not just in Ethiopia, but in all of Africa.   *Nati, age 13 (Ethiopia)*

I want to do something important with my life that will honor my father and mother's name.
Endriyas, age 13 (Ethiopia)

I want to make a difference in the world. I want to help people living on the street. *Tigist, age 9 (Ethiopia)*

I want to help with their vision. *Alexandra, age 18 (USA)*

I hope the other people will come to Ethiopia to share our world with us. *Tadelech, age 14 (Ethiopia)*

I want to work with people with HIV/AIDS. I want to get people from other countries involved, and create homes and places for people to live and work.
Meskerem, age 13 (Ethiopia)

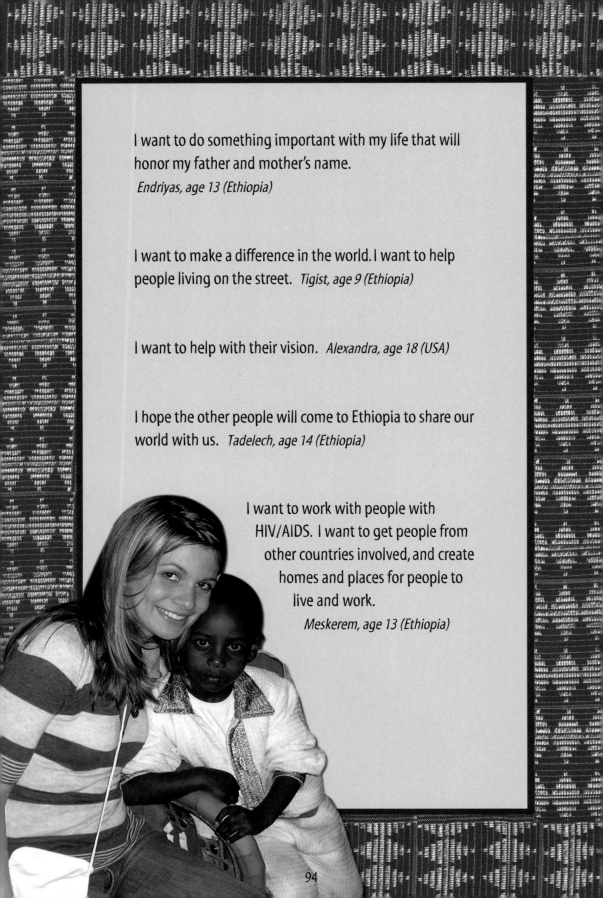

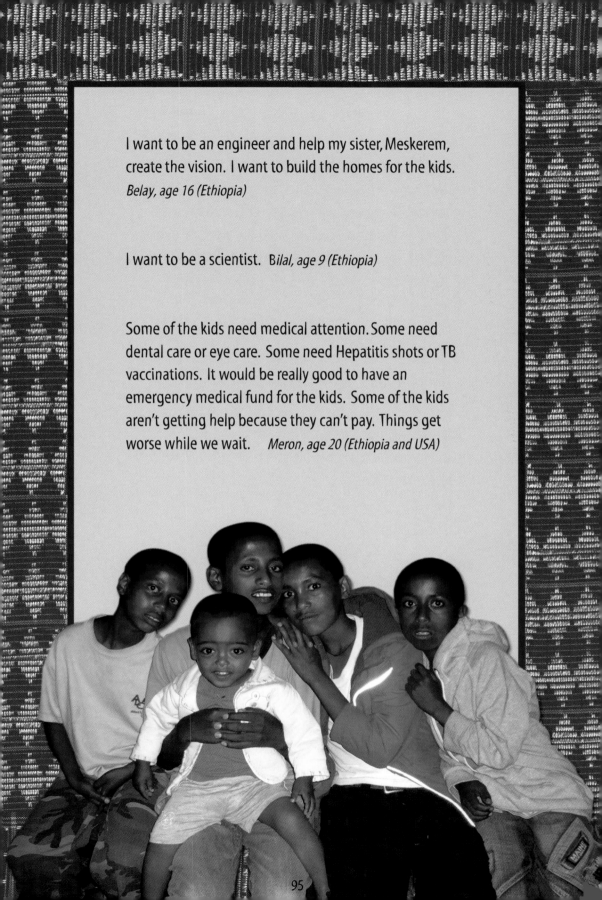

I want to be an engineer and help my sister, Meskerem, create the vision. I want to build the homes for the kids.
Belay, age 16 (Ethiopia)

I want to be a scientist. *Bilal, age 9 (Ethiopia)*

Some of the kids need medical attention. Some need dental care or eye care. Some need Hepatitis shots or TB vaccinations. It would be really good to have an emergency medical fund for the kids. Some of the kids aren't getting help because they can't pay. Things get worse while we wait. *Meron, age 20 (Ethiopia and USA)*

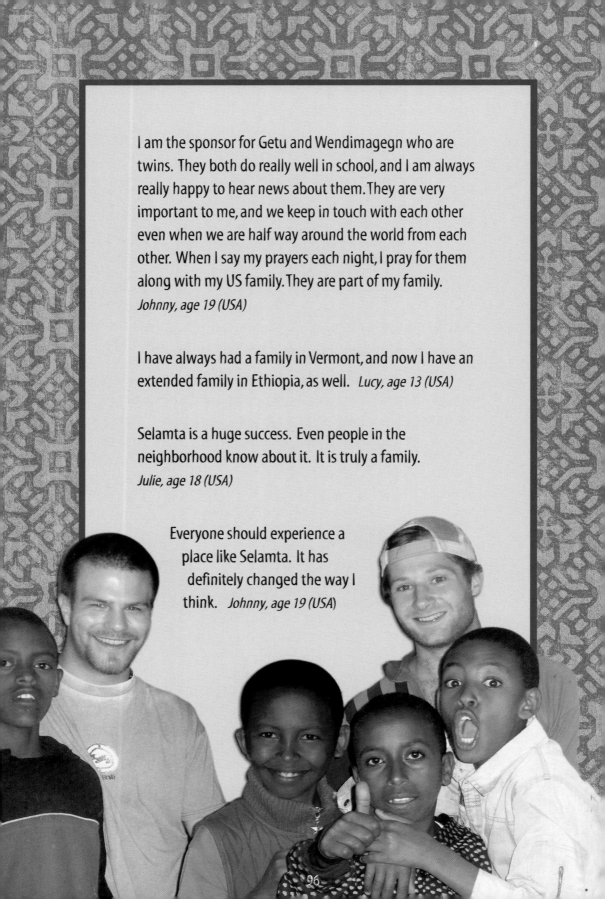

I am the sponsor for Getu and Wendimagegn who are twins. They both do really well in school, and I am always really happy to hear news about them. They are very important to me, and we keep in touch with each other even when we are half way around the world from each other. When I say my prayers each night, I pray for them along with my US family. They are part of my family.
Johnny, age 19 (USA)

I have always had a family in Vermont, and now I have an extended family in Ethiopia, as well. *Lucy, age 13 (USA)*

Selamta is a huge success. Even people in the neighborhood know about it. It is truly a family.
Julie, age 18 (USA)

Everyone should experience a place like Selamta. It has definitely changed the way I think. *Johnny, age 19 (USA)*

It was difficult to leave Ethiopia. I thought that it would be a relief, going back to America where running water and electricity were standard. But, all I could think about was how much I was going to miss everything about Ethiopia when I left. I would miss the sights, sounds, smells, and most of all, the people that I met in Ethiopia. I am not generally one to cry, but I balled my eyes out when I had to leave my friends. *Ben, age 21 (USA)*

Once I had been at Selamta for a long time, it became very hard to be away from the kids. I think about them every day. Sometimes at college when I am taking notes, I start to doodle, and I write lists of the kids I want to remind myself to send letters to, or items I think they might need. I keep a framed picture of my sponsor girls, Meseret and Lidet by my bedside so I can always see their smiling faces. Being at Selamta is a very rewarding experience because you know you are making a difference in these children's lives. But I have been rewarded in more ways than you know-I've made lifetime friends and family.
Robyn, age 21 (USA)

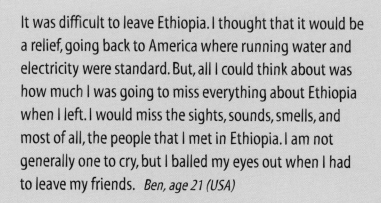

It was really painful to say good-bye when I had to leave to come back to the United States. The kids are so loving and giving. It is interesting to me that the kids at Selamta have so much less than most American kids, yet they are much more willing to share what they have. They also give of themselves.   *Johnny age 19 (USA)*

I consider both the US and Ethiopia home, and both family.   *Meron, age 20 (Ethiopia and USA)*

We need people who are willing to come to Ethiopia and help those children who are still living on the streets. People like "Mom."   *Fitsum, age 16 (Ethiopia)*

I believe they should come here and see the wonderful places like Lalibela. These are a part of my Ethiopia.
Getu, age 15 (Ethiopia)

I want to pass a message to the world. I know the world knows Ethiopia, not for its good things, but for its poverty. I know this because people have told me this before. I want to invite people to come and visit Ethiopia to see what is here. I want people to understand the culture and the land. They will change their minds about Ethiopia.
Teddy, age 16 (Ethiopia)

If every person helps just one other person, the world will change.
Fitsum, age 16 (Ethiopia)

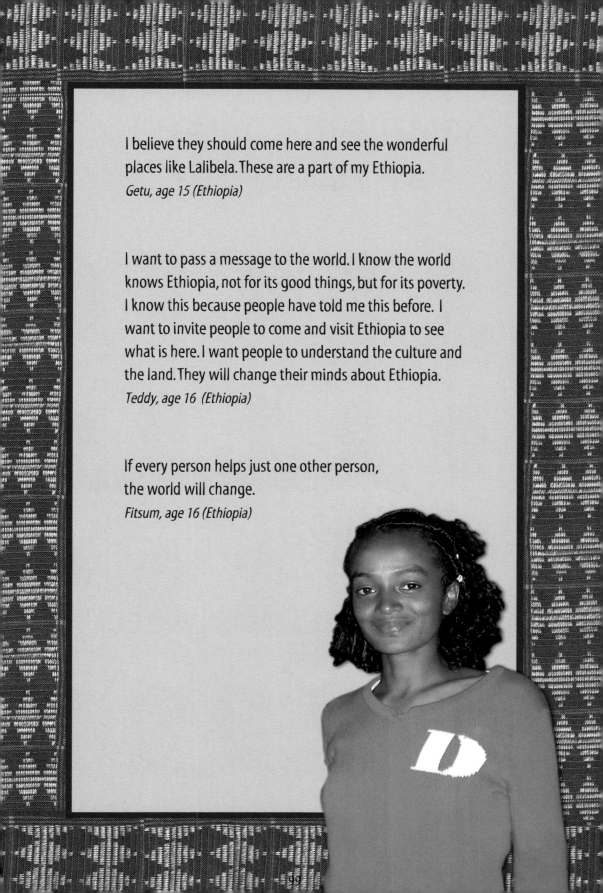

Selamta's Children
Addis Ababa, Ethiopia

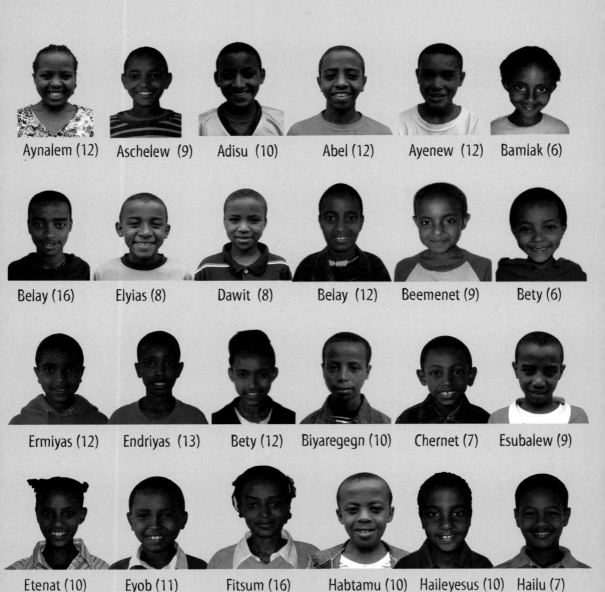

Aynalem (12) Aschelew (9) Adisu (10) Abel (12) Ayenew (12) Bamlak (6)

Belay (16) Elyias (8) Dawit (8) Belay (12) Beemenet (9) Bety (6)

Ermiyas (12) Endriyas (13) Bety (12) Biyaregegn (10) Chernet (7) Esubalew (9)

Etenat (10) Eyob (11) Fitsum (16) Habtamu (10) Haileyesus (10) Hailu (7)

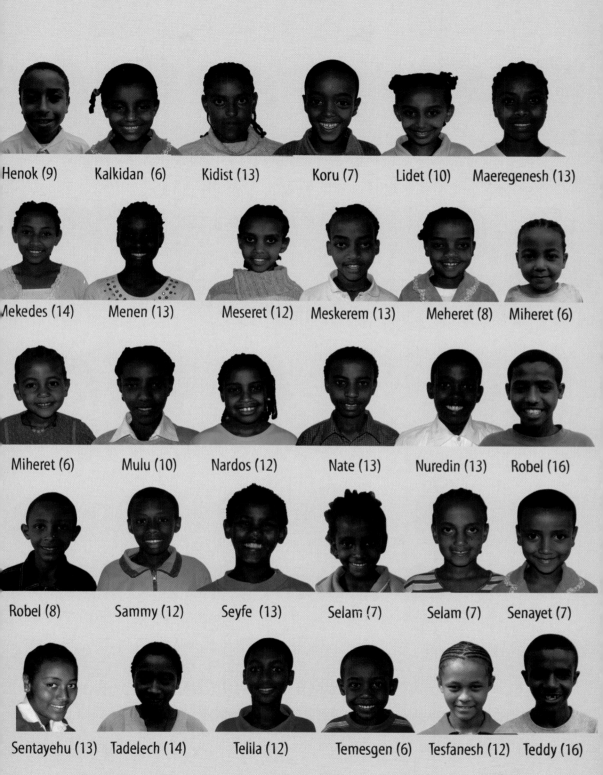

Henok (9) Kalkidan (6) Kidist (13) Koru (7) Lidet (10) Maeregenesh (13)

Mekedes (14) Menen (13) Meseret (12) Meskerem (13) Meheret (8) Miheret (6)

Miheret (6) Mulu (10) Nardos (12) Nate (13) Nuredin (13) Robel (16)

Robel (8) Sammy (12) Seyfe (13) Selam (7) Selam (7) Senayet (7)

Sentayehu (13) Tadelech (14) Telila (12) Temesgen (6) Tesfanesh (12) Teddy (16)

Tigist (9) Tigist (9) Tizita (9) Walelegn (10) Wendimagegn (15) Wondimagegn

Adelegn (14) Bilal (10) Bilal (10) Fetlework (14) Meheret (11) Mariyamawit (3)

Milion (10) Selam (16) Tefared (9) Tsion (2) Tsion (15) Tigist (10)

Tsega (2) Yordanos (15) Getu (15) Yohanes (11) Yohanes (11) Melena

"My heart is open wide tonight,
For stranger, kith or kin...

Selamta's Ambassadors
from the United States

Alexandra (18) Becky (18) Ben (21) Bethlehem (13) Brian (20) Chelsea (20)

Christopher (18) John (22) Johnny (19) Julie (18) Lucy (13) Margaret (18)

Michael (18) Meron (20) Robyn (21) Seth (20) Zoe (21) Camille (18)

Mike (21)

"I would not bar a single door
Where love might enter in."

From a traditional song, Author unknown

For more information about Selamta, contact
http://www.humancapitalfoundation.org/hcf/africa_selamta.guid